Martica K. Heaner, from Texas and Arizona, London. She has written six books and produced several fitness videos. She has been nominated for several fitness industry awards, and was made 1992 *National Fitness Leader of the Year* by the Fitness Professionals Association. Martica has a BA in English Literature and Exercise Science from Smith College in Massachusetts, and is certified by several international fitness teaching organisations. She writes on all aspects of health and fitness for many newspapers and magazines both in the US and the UK.

Also by Martica K. Heaner

The Squeeze
Curves – The Body Transformation Strategy
The 7 Minute Sex Secret
Secrets of an Aerobics Instructor
How to be a Personal Trainer

Eat More, Weigh Less

Martica K. Heaner

Illustrations by Chris Mutter

First published in Great Britain in 1998 by Hodder & Stoughton
A division of Hodder Headline PLC

A Coronet paperback

10 9 8 7 6 5 4 3 2 1

A CIP catalogue record for this title is available from the
British Library

ISBN 0 340 65760 X

Typeset by Hewer Text Composition Services, Edinburgh

Printed and bound in Great Britain by Mackays of Chatham PLC

Hodder & Stoughton
A division of Hodder Headline PLC
338 Euston Road
London NW1 3BH

To Sister Anne Lenore, my teacher at St Francis Xavier School, whose science class inspired me at thirteen years old to limit sugar, opt for whole wheat bread, and make a conscious effort to eat more nutritious food. This, at a very formative time, when starvation, deprivation and an obsession with thinness were starting to become a way of life for most teenage girls.

To my mother who instilled her never-say-diet philosophy in me.

And especially to my grandmother, whose genius cooking has always included the freshest of vegetables, an abundant supply of sumptuous fruit and her special skill for making everything taste delicious.

ACKNOWLEDGEMENTS

Thank you to Penny Hunking SRD, accredited sports dietician and director of Energise, who gave valuable advice on the nutritional aspects of this book. Thank you also to my agent, Darley Anderson, and Rowena Webb, Laura Brockbank and Camilla Sweeney at Hodder & Stoughton.

CONTENTS

PART THREE

FOREWORD

Being overweight, and even obese, is a growing problem in the UK. Many people have the problem of either eating too little healthy food or too much unhealthy food, both of which can result in weight gain. Many people also fail to eat the right variety of foods necessary to provide all the nutrients in the right balance or in sufficient quantities.

The only permanent approach to losing fat and staying well is through nutritious, low-fat eating combined with increased activity. The concepts delivered in *Eat More, Weigh Less* address these issues and can help enable you to eat lots, enjoy your food, while achieving a healthy body weight too. Read and enjoy!

Penny Hunking, SRD, PEA, RSA,
Accredited Sports Dietician

PART ONE

STOP DENYING YOURSELF

- Do you find that no matter what you eat, or don't eat, you *still* seem to slowly gain weight?
- Are you tired of being your own 'food police' – monitoring every morsel you put in your mouth and feeling guilty for slipping up?
- Have you noticed your stomach or thighs getting bigger or less toned?
- Are you starting to accumulate more cellulite in problem areas?
- Does getting back into shape seem to get more and more difficult?

If you don't *look* or *feel* as good as you want to, this book will show you how to use food and movement to nourish and stimulate your body.

The secret to achieving the body you want, and feeling good in it, is to eat enough of the right foods and to stay active. Everybody instinctively knows this. But putting it into practice is another story because *exactly* what to eat and what exercise to do is not always clear.

There are many conflicting ideas around concerning what to eat, and most diet regimes are hard to stick to.

It's unrealistic to think that you can resist indulging every now and then, when eating out, fast foods and pre-packaged meals are such a major part of modern life.

Staying active is even more difficult: you may not have the time to work out, or you may not enjoy it. And if you've exercised before, but found it didn't change your body shape much, it's understandably hard to motivate yourself to do it again.

Keeping lean is much easier than you might realise, as long as you follow a few simple guidelines. *Eat More, Weigh Less* will show you how to win the battle of the bulge by manipulating the ways your body uses and stores the food you eat.

SPEED UP YOUR METABOLISM

The key to weight loss is your metabolism. How you eat, what you eat, and the exercise you do all affect your metabolism and how much fat is stored. Once you learn how your metabolism works, and how to keep it revved up, you can enjoy food without guilt: you can eat more and weigh less.

Your metabolism is like a motor that keeps your body running. It needs a certain amount of fuel each day. The fuel it uses is the food stored in your body. Each unit of energy is known as a calorie. When you eat, food is converted into calories that your body then uses for energy.

The faster your metabolism is, the more calories you burn, which means that you can eat more. The slower it is, the easier it is for you to gain weight. The calories you eat that don't get used become stored as fat on your bottom, thighs, abdomen and other areas of the body, for future use. Many people have too much fat so they diet to try to lose it.

Reversing Your Metabolism

But as you may have experienced before, losing weight from dieting is easy – the problem is keeping it off. This is because eating less can both deprive you of nutrients and slow your metabolism. The lack of nutrients saps your energy levels and makes your body function poorly. The slowed metabolism is the bane of anyone trying to lose weight because it traps you in a vicious cycle:

eat less → lose weight (and muscle) → metabolism slows down to compensate → gain weight (often ending up heavier than you were to start with)

When you diet without exercising, most of the weight you lose is muscle. Because the weight you gain back after dieting is often *fat*, not muscle, you also end up flabbier and fatter than you were originally. To further complicate matters, after the age of 25, you lose half a pound of muscle mass a decade. This may not seem like much, but in terms of your metabolism, it means you need fewer calories for energy each day – now eating the same amount that you used to can cause you to gain weight. In terms of the way you look, you lose muscle tone and increase fat in your problem areas. The natural ageing process contributes to slowing your metabolism even more and traps you in a downward spiral.

Usually, with each passing year, the less active you become – sitting at a desk, in a car, or lounging on the sofa – the less calories you burn. In other words, *if you don't use it, you lose it*. An increasingly sedentary lifestyle causes you to lose even more vital muscle mass. The less muscle you have, the slower your metabolism becomes, making it easier to gain fat.

This is why you can suddenly end up with middle-age spread – you become fatter and less firm than you ever were, even though you may not have changed your lifestyle much. In fact, now you may even be *more* careful of what you eat. Eating too little, or eating the wrong things, as well as not exercising, or not doing enough of the right exercise, can reverse your metabolism and slow it down.

The effects are far-reaching. Not only does a worsened physical state bruise your self-confidence, it can also have damaging implications for all aspects of your health: an increased risk of many diseases including heart disease, cancer and osteoporosis, as well as less structural support for your body, making you more susceptible to pain from a bad back, weak knees or arthritis. You may feel more tired, your sex drive may decrease, and of course, you gain weight so much more easily.

But this is preventable, if you act now. It is possible to speed up your metabolism to help keep your weight under control and to stay feeling energetic as you grow older.

Losing Weight

Studies show that the only way to *permanently* lose weight is to exercise along with following a healthy eating plan. In this way you nourish yourself *and* speed up your metabolism. When you eat well, you have the energy to exercise. More importantly, a well-fed brain leaves you in a positive mental state to *want* to exercise.

Exercise burns extra calories and replaces the muscle that you've lost from dieting or from being inactive in the past. More muscle means you can eat more, because muscle is very active tissue. The more you have, the more calories you need and the higher your metabolism is. That's why very fit people can eat loads while others seem to just *look* at a piece of cake and gain weight.

Eating Well Speeds Up Your Metabolism

Your body not only needs fuel in the form of calories to work efficiently; it also needs other nutrients such as vitamins, minerals and other substances. These are the life-giving components of foods. When you do not get enough calories or nutrients, your body cannot run smoothly because every physiological process is impaired. Your body cannot make the proper enzymes, proteins or hormones that it needs. It cannot repair cell walls or strengthen the immune system which helps you fight illness.

An inadequate supply of the substances your body needs to operate can also hamper your ability to digest, store and use the food you eat. Fat and carbohydrate breakdown, as well as proper absorption of the nutrients that you do eat, can be hindered. Hormone regulation can be thrown off kilter, often causing you to gain weight. When your body cannot use and produce energy effectively, your metabolism is affected.

This in turn affects your ability to *increase* your metabolism. You don't have the mental motivation or physical energy to exercise, so you don't. Your body instinctively senses that it needs more fuel so you develop cravings for what I call 'dead' food: food that is low in life-giving nutrients. These foods are usually calorie-dense, or fattening. You get full on them quickly, leaving little room or inclination to eat the foods that will provide the energy and all the nutrients you need. This further weakens you. You become lethargic and tired, mentally and physically.

What you eat and how you eat can, however, speed up your metabolism. Carbohydrates such as rice and vegetables require more energy to be digested than fats such as cheese or cream. Eating smaller, more frequent meals also requires more energy since the digestive system is working more often. Eating much more nutrient-rich food will ensure that you feel satiated, not hungry all the time. The vitamins, minerals and other properties in these foods will enable your body to operate at its maximum. This means you'll digest better, you'll be better equipped to metabolise your fat, and you'll have more energy. Following these and other smart eating techniques will affect your metabolism and help you to lose weight without dieting.

The right food is vital to a healthy, energetic life and so you should eat *more* of it, not less.

Activity Speeds Up Your Metabolism

When you're active, your muscles work harder than normal. This requires energy. So when you move, you burn more calories. This is vital for permanent weight loss because being active uses up much of the fat that is stored at different fat storage sites on your body like the hips, abdomen and thighs. There are several ways to become more active and speed up your metabolism.

1. You can simply become a little busier throughout your day. The more you move around, whether it's getting up and out of your chair more often, using the stairs, or doing more errands, the more calories your body will burn. This kind of activity sneaks more exercise into your life, but without too much effort. For overall health and general weight control, this amount of activity is fine. But to lose weight and keep your body toned, it is not enough.

2. You can also do concentrated bouts of 'fat-burning' exercise such as walking, playing tennis, cycling or aerobics. When your body moves vigorously for 15 or 20 minutes, it draws upon its energy stores to produce the calories it needs to move. The more calories you burn, the more fat you lose. High-energy exercise can boost your metabolism temporarily (you can burn up to 600 calories an hour doing this, and slightly more than you would at rest in the few hours after exercise). Your overall health will improve dramatically if you incorporate this type of cardiovascular exercise, and you will speed up the weight-loss process by burning more calories faster.

3. For long-term weight control you can do slower, controlled resistance exercises which target specific muscles in the legs, arms or torso. These do not use up a high number of calories at one time, however, because it doesn't take that much energy to bend and straighten your leg, for example, in comparison to running down the street. But these exercises have the

potential to boost your metabolism permanently because they build strength and tone. These exercises replace the muscle you have lost from past diets and a sedentary lifestyle.

The more muscle your body has, the more calories you use *all the time*. Resistance exercises – most effectively performed with weights – are often overlooked, especially by women who are afraid of becoming musclebound. But these are crucial to weight control. By increasing the muscle in your body, you will enable yourself to eat more because you'll naturally burn more calories than you used to.

The 28-day *Eat More, Weigh Less* plan is based on these principles. By speeding up your metabolism and fuelling yourself with nutrient-rich foods you can decrease fat and control your weight.

WEIGHT vs. FAT

Body weight can be deceiving, because people come in all shapes and sizes. Although the food you eat and the level of activity in your daily life can affect the way you look, you are born with a basic body shape. Your specific shape is predetermined by genetics. If your parents are tall and thin, chances are you will be too. Even if you gain weight, your underlying frame will still be that of a tall, thin person.

There are three body types based on limb length, muscular development and body fat distribution. These classic body shapes are known as the endomorph, mesomorph and ectomorph – more commonly known as the pear, hourglass and rectangle shapes. Two people can be the same height and weight, but be a totally different *shape*. In addition, one person can *look* heavier but weigh less, while another can look lighter but weigh more. Superfit people often look lean, but weigh more on the scales because they have dense muscle mass; while another person who is a perfect size 10 and weighs 8 stone still doesn't look very good because she has no muscle tone. You can be underweight, but have a high percentage of fat. This is why some thin people still have cellulite, which is simply fat stored just underneath the skin at the common fat sites on the hips and thighs.

Your overall weight doesn't really say that much about how you look. But many women still rely on weight loss from dieting to improve body shape. Being skinnier won't make you look better if you're not physically fit, and your body shape may stay exactly the same. Dieters lose weight from the upper body first so a pear-shaped woman may still look out of proportion after a weight-loss diet if she does not exercise.

To improve the way you look, your aim should not be to lose *overall weight*, but to lose *fat weight*. Overall body weight used to be the standard way to assess fatness. But scales are inaccurate because they also measure the amount of water, muscle, bone and other tissues in your body. Scales are also a poor indicator of overall health.

A better measure of body shape is your fat weight, or percentage of body fat and muscle in comparison to your overall weight. You will look the leanest if you have a high percentage of muscle and low percentage of body fat: 16 to 25 per cent is the optimal percentage of body fat for most adult women. A healthy range of body fat for men is between 10 and 20 per cent. Although you may not know your own body fat percentage, if you feel flabby and weak, chances are you have a higher percentage of body fat and a lower percentage of muscle mass than you should.

Fat Isn't All Bad

Extra fat isn't always a health risk – where it's stored is key. Dimply, subcutaneous fat, just underneath the skin, is healthier than excess visceral fat which is stored deep near the organs. Studies show that apple-shaped bodies with more abdominal fat have a greater susceptibility to obesity-related diseases than those with lower body fat in the hips and thighs. Women have more sex-specific fat, typically stored in the lower body: this is related to their child-bearing role.

Some body fat is crucial to good health. Fat is the body's main energy source: it is needed for the proper functioning of many body systems including the central nervous system. Your body draws upon its fat stores as fuel for all physiological processes including cell repair and cell duplication. Over 50 per cent of the calories your body uses for everyday functions like eating, sleeping, thinking, digestion and exercise, come from fat. For women, it provides the extra energy needed for reproduction and proper hormone functions (which is why they have more of it). Fat also provides warmth for the organs. Body fat that is too low is unhealthy. A woman with less than 16 per cent body fat may stop menstruating.

Why Do Some People Look Fatter Than Others?

A person is born with a predetermined amount of fat cells. Heredity predisposes some people to have a higher number of fat cells than others. Your genes also determine where your fat cells are distributed. Although there are individual differences between all people, in general men and women carry their extra weight in different places. Men tend to store fat primarily in their abdominal and chest areas. Women tend to store fat on their thighs, hips, breasts and abdomen. Height will determine how well you carry fat; tall people with long limbs can get away with extra fat whereas short people tend to look heavier with a few extra pounds.

The total number of fat cells stays constant except during the early stages of childhood, in adolescence, pregnancy and in extreme cases of obesity. Generally, when you gain or lose weight, rather than multiplying, your fat cells grow bigger or smaller. Unfortunately it is impossible to control which fat stores are used (in the thighs, for example), and which are not (in the breasts). When you lose weight, research has shown that fat is lost first from the upper body and then later from the lower body. In women, lower body fat is more resilient and harder to lose because of its important biological role.

Spot Reducing Doesn't Work

If you stick to an exercise and healthy eating plan, you will probably see a decrease in fat from your abdomen, thighs and other problem areas. But there are certain characteristics which you may not be able to alter. Many people do exercises such as abdominal crunches and leg lifts to lose fat from certain body parts. But these exercises will not result in lost inches because muscle conditioning works the muscle, not the fat, in that area. Fat calories *are* burned in order to supply the energy to work the muscle, but these exercises require such a minimal amount of energy (not much more than watching television) that they don't make much of a dent in your fat stores. For a long-term approach to shaping your body, performing these exercises with weights will help replace lost muscle, helping to firm up the area and ultimately boosting your overall metabolism.

Losing Body Fat

Eating the right foods will help prevent your body from storing extra fat, and will encourage it to draw upon its fat stores. Exercise will help use even more fat from these stores.

You must include both types of exercise: resistance training where you strengthen specific muscles, and aerobic training where you move your whole body, not just a single muscle. This requires more effort and therefore burns more calories.

Although you cannot control which fat cells are targeted, generally, when you lose fat, it is taken from fat sites all over the body. In the initial stages of a diet and exercise programme, you may become smaller all over, but still retain an unbalanced pear or apple shape. If you continue the healthier, active lifestyle over a long period, the fat from the harder-to-lose areas will eventually be used.

What you eat and when you eat also determines how much fat you carry. Although the total number of calories you eat will affect your weight, studies show that eating a diet high in fat calories compared to a diet high in carbohydrate calories will result in more of the fat being stored in your body, rather than used for energy immediately. Your body also runs by a special biological clock which regulates the timing of all its physiological processes. It is most active during the day, so food you eat earlier is digested better. By eating most of your food, and especially more fattening foods, early, rather than late in the evening, you can affect how much fat is stored in your body.

It's important to remember that your *overall* eating and exercise habits determine how successful you are. You didn't gain extra weight from one or two fattening meals, but from a pattern of them over a period of time. Similarly, you won't lose weight from dieting one month a year if you return to poor eating the rest of the time. Nor will you improve your body shape if you only exercise sporadically.

Whether it's food or fitness, it's more effective to do a little consistently on a regular basis, rather than a lot for a limited period.

Translating Fat Loss Into Weight Loss

When you lose fat weight, it may not always show up on the scale. Sometimes you can even gain weight from the replaced muscle – even though you look much leaner and toned. But don't panic – weight loss on the scale is not what it seems, and is usually regained quickly. If you keep your metabolism boosted with lots of the right foods and regular activity, over time your fat loss will register as weight loss on the scale.

Losing one pound of fat looks very different from losing one pound of weight. For example, the scales can show that you have lost five pounds in one day from fasting or sweating, but your body will not look different because you have lost five pounds of water, muscle and other tissues, in addition to a bit of fat. When losing five pounds of pure fat, however, your body registers actual inch loss and a decrease in cellulite, bumps and lumps as the fat stores are used up. Your body shape – including problem areas – looks leaner.

To lose one pound of fat you need to burn between 3,500 and 4,000 calories above your daily energy requirements. If you were to try to use this many calories through exercise, it would take about eight hours of intense workouts. So you can see that it is physiologically impossible to burn this amount of fat in a few days. But by taking a long-term approach you can spread it out, and lower your fat weight. All you need to do is increase your daily activity, make your exercise more efficient so that you burn the maximum amount of calories during the time you spend working out, and include muscle-replacing exercises in your routine. The bonus is that the longer you stick to it, the greater the benefits. You'll speed up your metabolism so that losing fat and controlling weight becomes even easier.

WHY EATING LESS DOESN'T WORK

Many people opt for dieting to lose weight. Indeed cutting out 1,000 or so calories of food a day is much faster than using up that number of calories through exercise.

There are many ways you can eat less. You can:

- eat a high-carbohydrate, low-fat diet (lots of rice cakes and dry baked potatoes)
- follow a high-protein diet (lots of boiled chicken and egg whites)
- food-combine – never eating fruit with other foods, or proteins and carbohydrates together
- eat pre-packaged calorie-controlled frozen dinners
- use artificially flavoured chocolate diet drinks
- cut out dairy products or wheat
- slurp clear watery soup made from as few ingredients as possible
- even eat only ice-cream for two weeks – as much as you want.

All of these diets will help you lose weight. Most do so because they make you eat less. Sometimes this is obvious. Cabbage soup and diet drinks clearly restrict your calories. You'll also eat less when you're made conscious of how much you actually eat. So physically tabulating your portion sizes, calories and fat grams encourages you to eat less.

But sometimes the fact that you're 'dieting' is disguised. Instead your weight loss is attributed to some mystical element of the diet. Some diets claim that the weight loss is due to pseudo-scientific but unproven theories. Food-combining advocates describe the result of mixing two uncomplementary foods: seemingly innocent items like a chicken sandwich or fruit with your cereal will rot in your gut, they say. Who wants to eat after hearing that? Of course you'll eat less, especially if the theory means there's not much you can eat unless you stay at home and combine your food the right way all the time.

If you're like most women, and increasing numbers of men, you've been on several of these or other diets in your life. You may have lost weight, but it was probably just temporary. And when you gained it back, you added a few extra pounds for your trouble.

The Life of a Dieter

That's the way dieting works. You follow the traditional formula for weight loss: you eat less. But in a world full of fattening fast-foods, it's a struggle. You must become obsessed about what you can and cannot eat. You must religiously count calories or figure out the percentage of your fats that are saturated. You must remember which foods are bad and avoid them. Or you must weigh and record every morsel you put into your mouth.

So on a 'good' day, when you've fastidiously followed all the rules of your diet, you end up eating a piece of plain toast, three rice cakes, half an ounce of grilled fish, an iceberg lettuce salad and a dry baked potato.

On a 'good' week, you have a neat little food diary listing everything you ate, the time you ate it and, if you're especially meticulous, the portion sizes, calories and number of fat grams. You live a life of denial, but you feel proud and virtuous for it. You successfully turned down crisps at the pub. You turned down the second helping of vegetables at the dinner party. You were able to abstain from the biscuits in the kitchen, the ice-cream in the freezer and the whole milk in your coffee.

And rightly so, because when you take your weekly step on to the scales, you find that you have lost a few pounds. You record this in your diet diary. You tell your friends. You measure and re-measure your waist. You try on that old pair of too-tight trousers to see if they're looser. You use this carrot as motivation to stick to the diet. And it works for a while. But there are problems with this scenario.

At some point, you have to return to your real life. Other things will take up time, like your family, your friends and your career. You will go to places where Ryvita and rice cakes are not available. You will be served dishes where protein and carbohydrates are inseparable. You will forget – or not have the time – to write down what you eat. Or you'll just get tired of denying yourself – you'll lose the will to eat less, and binge. Then you'll feel that these slip-ups are moments of weakness.

Ultimately, eating less cripples you mentally. Food becomes the most important thing in your life. Most of your waking hours are spent thinking about it – either planning what you will eat, commending yourself on what you did eat, talking yourself out of what you want to eat or feeling guilty about the 'bad' food you stuffed your face with. Food is meant to be nourishment, the sustenance of life, but suddenly it becomes a weapon. Not only are you obsessed with it, you are afraid of it. Food represents everything you don't want to be: fat, unattractive, flabby, undesired and unhappy.

The irony is that if you have this attitude, you may not even be aware of the negative influence food has on your life. Like the anorexic who looks in the mirror and sees fat, a chronic dieter sees life-giving food as life-destroying. Someone who is always mentally calculating their calories, scouring the supermarket aisles for the fat-free options, or avoiding food at social events because it doesn't meet their rigid requirements, doesn't realise that it's not healthy to think like this.

Women, of course, have greater social pressure to be thin and beautiful, so food obsession is a part of most women's lives. In the same nonchalant way that men talk about sports, women recite to each other exactly what they've eaten that day. Any man can tell you of the many women he has known who will only pick at a salad at dinner, refuse dessert and talk about how fat they feel. A friend of mine relates the story of the time he picked up a girl for their first date. He asked her which restaurant she wanted to go to. She said that she'd rather not go to one, as she didn't like to eat in public.

And men are becoming increasingly obsessed by food as well. Especially those who have been overweight before and are desperate not to gain the weight back. But controlling your diet as a way of controlling your life will backfire in several ways.

The More You Diet, the Fatter You Get

Eating less cripples you physically as well as mentally. Your body will function poorly if the food you eat does not satisfy your nutritional requirements. From a weight-loss perspective, eating less and losing weight can make you fatter.

If your diet is too drastic, unbalanced or rigid, or if you don't exercise, you will probably regain the weight once you stop the diet. The weight you lose will be fat and muscle. The weight you gain back will be fat. You end up with less muscle so you're flabbier. With less muscle, your metabolism slows down. So now you may gain even more weight from eating normal amounts of food.

Years of on-again, off-again dieting, a lifetime spent trying to eat less, will make you weigh more. You'll get fatter and flabbier – which defeats the whole purpose of dieting.

Of course you never realise this at the beginning. You're full of hopes and expectations about the thin hips and thighs, flat stomach and new you that will emerge. But study after study has shown that traditional dieting is a waste of time. Everyone knows that the 10 pounds you can lose in a week from a crash diet is simply water. Your body shape doesn't change and the minute you drink and eat normally again, the scales tip back to the usual reading.

Fast fat loss is physiologically impossible: it takes time. And most people give up their healthy eating and exercise plans long before they reap the rewards. Studies show that almost 70 per cent of those who start a diet will drop out within six weeks. Even those ultra-disciplined types who manage to stick it out ultimately fail. Over 90 per cent of those who lose weight from a diet will gain it back within a year. Don't let 'success' stories fool you. Diet gurus who splash 'before and after' pictures of men and women who have followed their particular regime never show you the 'after-after' pictures when they've gained all their lost weight back. Dieting is a waste of time. You will gain nothing but weight and hunger pains.

Even though depriving yourself of food will help you lose weight temporarily, realistically it's not the best way to lose weight permanently. And eating less won't make you look or feel better, as you'll find out from this book.

If you are accustomed to dieting and have suffered many years forcing yourself to eat less, you can reverse this cycle. You can look and feel better than you ever have before. And you can eat.

WARNING SIGNS

Most people diet because they want to look better. But the way you look and feel is dependent on much more than just being fat or thin. What good is a flat stomach if you have spots on your face, dark circles under your eyes and bruises on your thighs? What good is fitting into a pair of size 8 trousers if you're too tired to go out?

Experts agree that the way to maintain your weight is to eat a high-carbohydrate, low-fat diet while monitoring the overall calories you consume. Many people successfully follow these recommendations. On any given day they may eat a plain baked potato, dry toast, a bagel, a diet cola and a salad.

But the surprise is this: although these foods will help you maintain, or even lose weight, this is not a highly nutritious diet. A day of these seemingly healthy food choices may create as much of a nutritional deficiency as eating a hamburger, a chocolate shake and french fries. This is because the quality of the food you eat – regardless of its fat, protein or carbohydrate content – dramatically affects how well your body operates. This, in turn, affects how you look and feel.

Everyone knows that junk food deprives you of crucial vitamins and minerals. But did you know that most low-calorie diets, or those that emphasise rigid food combinations, can also deprive you of vital nutrients? It's common for people who lose weight on a diet to feel tired, have headaches, a poor complexion and a lack of energy. Being skinny doesn't mean you'll look or feel any better; you could look and feel worse. Feeling sluggish means you'll be less active. Since regular exercise is the only way to keep the weight off, and prevent the loss of muscle mass that occurs with dieting, you are likely to gain your weight back and become flabbier in the process if your diet is lacking in nutrients.

A nourishing diet consists of adequate amounts of vitamins, minerals, carbohydrates, proteins, fibre, fats, water and even 'phytochemicals' – unidentified essential nutrients present in plant foods. Studies have determined the recommended daily allowances of most of these substances to ensure adequate nutrient intake. But many people don't even get close to the amount of nutrients they should be eating. And it's not only those who live on chips, crisps and soft drinks who are missing out. You could be living on a low-fat diet of baked potatoes, pasta, cottage cheese and salad, and still be suffering from a nutrient deficiency.

Chart 1:
Warning Signs of Nutritional Deficiencies

Your body	*Your emotions*
tired	depression
over-fat	increased anxiety
dull eyes	burnout
fatigued muscles	mood swings
pale complexion	irritability
spotty skin	
weak nails	*Your mind*
low sex drive	poor memory
poor sleep	headaches
bruise easily	increased stress
dry, scaly skin	poor concentration
thin hair	
dry hair	*Your health*
hair loss	weakened immune system
muscle cramping	increase in colds & minor
slow healing of wounds	illnesses
skin rashes	bone loss
sensitivity to bright light	low energy levels
feeling abnormally cold	anaemia
cracks at the corners of your	canker sores (or mouth ulcers)
mouth	menstrual cramps
	bleeding gums

How Nutrients in Food Affect You

Nutrient intake has an incredibly strong impact on your
vitality. Although the calories and fat you eat play a role,
the most important factor in how your body runs, and
therefore how well it metabolises fat, is how well-
nourished you are. You've heard the saying that beauty
comes from within. What you eat and put in your body
will mould how you look and feel. When you are not

27

eating enough of the right foods, you may suffer from poor skin, hair and nails, a lack of energy, depression, inability to concentrate and overall weakness.

Luckily, your body gives you clues long before nutritional deficiencies turn into serious health problems. Areas of the body you can see and feel will show outward signs that there is a problem. Some of these symptoms, such as poor sleep, chronic tiredness and problem skin, are so common that most people have no idea that the cause is simply poor eating and that they can control it. Eastern medicine has recognised this for centuries. One of the main criteria for diagnosing illnesses is to inspect various parts of the body such as the tongue, the breath, the smell, the pulse, the skin and the eyes for symptoms. You are walking proof of how well you've fuelled and taken care of your body.

It is not always easy to find a direct cause and effect relationship between food and physical ailment. Eating broccoli won't instantaneously cure acne, for example. This is because there is a variety of potential causes for most symptoms. Fatigue, for example, can be the result of several different vitamin or mineral deficiencies, and unless you get a professional, lengthy dietary analysis, it's not that easy to pinpoint what you're missing. But you can be assured that the better the food you put in your body, the better you will look and feel.

Chart 2:
The Food Guide Pyramid

Food group	Recommended daily servings	Sample serving
Vegetables	3–5	cup raw spinach, ½ cup steamed broccoli
Fruit	2–4	1 banana, orange or apple, ½ cup strawberries
Grains	6–11	½ cup cooked rice, ½ cup cooked oatmeal, 1 slice bread, ½ cup cooked pasta
Dairy	2–3	1 cup yoghurt, 1 cup milk, 1½oz cheese
Pulses, meat	2–3	½ cup cooked beans, 2oz meat, poultry or fish, 1 egg
Fats, oils & sweets	use sparingly	

1 cup = 8oz = 240ml

What Exactly Do You Need?

Most vitamins, minerals and other nutritional substances are needed in certain quantities if they are to fulfil their physiological function in the body. Nutritional research has determined the standard amounts the average person should eat in order to prevent nutrient deficiencies and many of the symptoms described in Chart 1. The most common figures are known as Recommended Daily Allowances (RDA).

Critics have argued that the RDAs are a guideline as to the *minimum* amount you should have to prevent problems, not the maximum amount you need to optimise your health. Nor do they take into account individual needs of different people. So the Department of Health has established new guidelines to better inform people of the minimum, optimum and maximum nutrient intakes. The Health Education Authority has compiled dietary advice for a broad range of individuals. These are known as Dietary Reference Values, or DRVs. Depending upon the nutrition, and research available detailing dosages, four categories of recommended requirements are given. These include the Estimated Average Requirement (EAR), the Reference Nutrient Intake (RNI), the Lower Reference Nutrient Intake (LRNI) and the Safe Intake. But don't worry, it's unnecessary to spend your time calculating the varying amounts of nutrient you are getting, as long as you eat well.

Eating nutritiously doesn't have to be complicated, however. Several professional research bodies have established guidelines to help determine exactly how much of different foods you should eat. The United States Department of Agriculture's Food Guide Pyramid (see above) shows how many servings of different food groups you should eat daily (e.g. 3–5 servings of vegetables; oils and fats sparingly; and 2–3 servings of beans, meat, poultry, dairy and fish). The American College of Sports Medicine advises that you eat at least 1,200 kilocalories per day, and more if you exercise. The UK Department of Health, Ministry of Agriculture, Fisheries and Food together with the Health Education Authority developed a graphic illustration called 'The

Balance of Good Health'. This is meant to show visually the proportions of foods that should be eaten. A plate is split into segments to represent the quantities of different food groups. According to this guideline, fruits and vegetables should comprise 33 per cent of the plate, grains, breads, potatoes and other cereals should comprise 33 per cent, milk and dairy foods 15 per cent, meat, fish and vegetarian alternatives 12 per cent, and food containing fat or sugar no more than 8 per cent of a person's daily calorie intake. By following these guidelines, which incorporate a variety of different foods and a minimum level of calories for energy, you can be assured that you will be meeting your minimal nutritional requirements without having to measure and calculate how many milligrams of each nutrient you are getting.

Can Supplements Help?

Some people prefer to take vitamins and other nutritional supplements. Experts vary on how helpful these actually are. Some nutritionists feel that supplements are excreted from the body and are just 'expensive urine'. Others believe that with deteriorating food quality and poor dietary habits, they can't hurt. Many studies show that nutritional supplements can help a variety of problems.

But there is no doubt that nutrients from real food are the preferred choice. Some supplements are not easily absorbed, and other nutrients that you may be taking can counteract each other. Most importantly, there are still many unidentified substances in food which are not available in supplement form, yet are crucial to good health. Most recently, food researchers have identified substances found in plant foods, the phytochemicals mentioned earlier. These are believed to have strong antioxidant properties.

So that you can nourish yourself properly, be aware of some of the many nutrients you need and the foods in which they are present.

Chart 3:
Nutrient Reference Guide

Nutrient	Deficiency symptoms	Eat more . . .
Protein	Dry, thin hair, grey skin	Grains, legumes, dairy, fish/meat
Folacin	Dry hair, ashen skin, weak nails, burning tongue, cracks in mouth	Legumes, spinach, greens, beans, cantaloupe, squash
Vitamin B12	Dry hair, weak nails, mood swings, anaemia	Meat, poultry, dairy, soybeans, mung beans, alfalfa, peas
Niacin	Irritability	Tuna, liver, chicken, mushrooms, peaches, peanuts, potatoes, cantaloupe, broccoli
Vitamin B6	Dry hair, cracks in corners of mouth, smooth tongue	Beans, potatoes, salmon, bananas, spinach, sunflower seeds, figs
Iron	Dry hair, fatigue, poor concentration, weakness, brittle nails, ridged or abnormally curved nails	Spinach, lentils, butterbeans, fish/poultry/meat with foods high in Vitamin C for best absorption

Nutrient Reference Guide

Nutrient	Deficiency symptoms	Eat more . . .
Vitamin C	Splitting, dry hair, easy bruising, bleeding gums	Oranges, grapefruit, broccoli, kiwi, strawberries, Brussels sprouts, mango, spinach, tomatoes
Vitamin A	Poor night vision, sensitivity to bright lights, dandruff, hair loss	Carrots, cantaloup, apricots, sweet potatoes, liver, spinach
Beta carotene	Rough skin, poor vision	Sweet potatoes, carrots, apricots
Biotin	Dry skin, hair loss, scaly skin, depression, muscle pain	Present in most foods
B vitamins	Tiredness, low energy levels, skin rashes, cracks in mouth, burning tongue, mood swings, depression	Green leafy vegetables, meats, beans
Water	Tiredness, irritability, headaches	Water, watery foods like juicy vegetables and fruits, e.g. watermelon
Linoleic acid	Flaky, dry skin	Vegetable oils, nuts and seeds
Vitamin B2	Poor vision, bloodshot eyes	Whole grains, milk, yoghurt
Vitamin E	Muscle cramping, dry skin	Vegetable oils, fruits, vegetables
Zinc	Slow wound healing, anorexia, hair loss, dry skin	Meat, wheat germ, spinach, peanuts, squash, greens, beans
Vitamin K	Rare, but inadequate blood clotting	Green leafy vegetables, cabbage, milk, liver

Nutrient Reference Guide

Nutrient	Deficiency symptoms	Eat more ...
Calcium	Bone loss	Milk, green vegetables, fish
Riboflavin	Skin rash around nose and lips, cracks at corners of mouth, dark red tongue	Liver, steak, mushrooms, milk, cottage cheese, spinach, broccoli, peaches, almonds, asparagus
Thiamine	Weakness	Brewer's yeast, sunflower seeds, green peas, black beans, watermelon, oatmeal, potatoes
Vitamin D	Weak bones, poor teeth, muscle spasms	Sunlight, milk
Potassium	Muscle spasms, excess sweating	Peaches, beans, squash, potatoes, spinach, peas, watermelon

LEARNING TO RECOGNISE 'DEAD' FOOD

Picture yourself coming home late at night.

You're starving. You had a cup of coffee at 4 p.m. but haven't eaten since. You ransack the cupboards and there's nothing you feel like eating. Some peas, a red pepper. Some potatoes, some tomatoes. It's late and you're too tired to cook. Then you spot the crisps. Just what you feel like. You wolf them down. The whole bag. All 1,500 calories and 85 fat grams of them. Since salt bloats you and fat satiates you, you feel full. You've quashed the stomach pangs and satisfied the craving. You don't feel hungry any more, so you don't bother eating a proper dinner.

Meanwhile, your body has just gone about nine hours without real food. Maybe much longer if your previous meal was low in nutrients. Your body is slowly being starved of vital nutrients. If you're tired, your immune system may be low and it needs those nutrients for fuel. If you have a virus lurking around, your weakened body is now prey to attack. And all because you gave in to impulse eating. Instead of slicing the tomatoes and red peppers, boiling the potatoes and eating *a few* of the crisps, you ate the whole bag and nothing else.

Too many people are used to succumbing to the

slovenly indulgence of cheap taste rather than appreciating fresh, natural fruits, vegetables, grains and beans. And the body suffers because of it. Stuffing yourself with *dead food* – processed, pre-packaged food that satisfies your taste buds, but provides little nutritionally – makes it easy to go for days without eating enough of the life-giving, nutrient-rich foods like fresh vegetables and fruit, whole grains and pulses. The busier you are, the easier this is to do because the modern lifestyle is not conducive to fuelling your body with the food that will make you feel and look your best. The need to conserve time and effort makes it easy to grab quick snacks and ready-to-eat foods without really knowing their contents.

Most people know they should eat better, but don't realise how poorly they really do eat. One apple a day is *not* enough to keep the doctor away. A ready-made meat pie is not your healthiest food option. Eating a baked potato and low-fat yoghurt all day is not enough. Not only is what you eat important, but so is the quantity and variety. If you eat better, you can eat more. This doesn't mean you have to cut out the 'bad' foods. You can eat the chocolate bar or crisps as long as you're fulfilling your primary nutritional needs.

Splurge, Don't Purge

If you're used to eating more junk food than you'd like, you can change your eating patterns. To get out of the trap of purging your body of nutrients, either by eating less (dieting) or eating worse, *splurge* on all the succulent, life-enhancing food you can. This may take a little readjustment because with the appeal of high-fat, highly processed sugary and salty foods, simple food seems much plainer and tasteless by comparison. This may also require a little re-education. As a vegetarian, the most frequent comment I receive is, 'What can you eat? Vegetables are so boring.' In fact, there are four times more kinds of vegetables than meat, and an equally varied number of ways to prepare them. But to the person who equates their vegetable intake for the week with iceberg lettuce, cucumber and tomato, the choice can seem very limited.

As well as retraining your palate, you may have to alter your mind-set. A common excuse for not eating well or exercising is 'I'd rather die young and have fun than be healthy and miserable.' Invariably the people who say this are always the most out of shape, unhealthy, alcohol- or drug-dependent people around. Their justification for not improving their lifestyle is that they're happy the way they are. But if they've never been in great shape physically or they've never been really well nourished, they have nothing to compare themselves to. They don't actually know what they're missing.

Compare your body and mind to an old junk car and a finely tuned sports car. In the perfect car you can notice when anything goes wrong. In order to keep it in good condition, you make an extra effort to take care of it. The junk car is so far gone it really doesn't matter how you treat it. But you can always improve how it runs by taking better care of it. The fact is, you'll have more energy, be more positive, be stronger and look better when you eat well and exercise.

The 4-Step Programme to Healthier Eating

To start eating more of the right foods and decrease your consumption of the unhealthier foods, follow these easy steps to make the transition smoother. Be realistic about how much you can change right away. Rather than trying to follow the perfect diet and abolish your habitual way of eating, take it one step at a time:

Observe

Continue your present eating habits, but analyse your diet. How can you modify it to incorporate better food choices? If you eat a sandwich at the same place for lunch every day, figure out what ingredients you can add or substitute to make it more nutritious. Identify areas where you can decrease the fat when it doesn't matter (i.e. eliminate the butter in your sandwich or ask for half the amount of cheese or mayonnaise).

Make small additions

Don't get drastic just yet. Make a few positive changes. Aim to eat one more vegetable a day. Keep fruit by your desk and nibble on that instead of the candy bar. Gradually adopt a few more positive choices so that while you still may have a partially unhealthy diet, you'll *also* have a healthy diet.

Don't worry about your weight just yet. Healthy foods tend to be low in fat so you can eat more without gaining weight. At this stage you're refuelling your body so it functions properly. When your brain and body are in tip-top shape, not only will you have the physical energy to exercise, you'll also feel happier and have a better self-image – that 10 pounds you'd like to lose won't seem as important. This will give you more emotional distance, so you can approach your weight concerns from a strong, confident mental position, and finally make a permanent change. When your body has all the right nutrients it will work properly so it will be easier for you to lose weight. You won't suffer from all these protective responses where your body is scrounging around trying to retain any calories it gets because it's not getting what it needs.

Substitute and reapportion

Keep up the healthy stuff and cut back on a few bad things. Substitute whole-fat milk with semi-skimmed or skimmed. Drink more water instead of coffee or soft drinks. Reapportion the ratios of the combinations of foods you eat. If you balance out your dishes in a smarter, healthier way and have more of the good things and less of the bad things, you'll be eating more 'real' food that will give you more energy and make you feel better. But you won't be missing out on the normal foods that are part of your everyday life; you won't be dieting. Eat vegetables with some pasta thrown in. Make a sandwich with more garnish than cheese.

Learning to love real food

The hardest thing about making a positive change in your lifestyle is not the giving up in itself but the elimination of your desire. You can only really change your behaviour by changing the impulses and attitudes which cause you to act in a certain way.

If you don't appreciate healthy food – how it tastes and how good it makes you feel – it will be much harder to improve your eating habits. It's difficult to force yourself to eat grains, beans and vegetables if you're not very interested in them. There is no sense cutting all the fat out of your diet if all you can do is envisage cream cakes and chips. Giving up something you really want makes you even more obsessed with it: 'I will not eat this, I will not eat this, I will not eat this'. This is mental torture. If you eat it and obsess about it, or don't eat it but still obsess about it, what's the real point of not eating it? You might as well eat it and enjoy it.

If what you're eating and its effect on your mental and physical health cease to be enjoyable, however, it will be easier for you to make smart eating choices. Consider the foods you eat. Rather than just stop eating junk, you need to achieve the mental state of not *wanting* to eat things that make you feel or look bad. The way to do this is to look at food from a different perspective.

When you have a craving for a poor food choice, consciously remind yourself that you want to treat your body with respect and make it feel good. Rather than thinking, 'I want the crisp, fried, greasy, salty taste of french fries in my full stomach', think, 'I want to put something in my body that will make me feel fresh, alive and energetic, not sluggish and lethargic and depressed.'

With time, your preference for fresh, healthy foods will become natural. You'll lose the cravings for junk. Studies have shown that the lower in fat your diet is, the less you crave it. The more nutritious food you eat, the better you'll feel, and the more nutritious food you'll want.

Healthy food only seems less exciting and flavoursome because you may have become addicted to bad foods. Once you break the addiction, however, some of the foods that you used to think were so delicious will seem unbearably unpalatable.

Are You a Victim of Poor Food Choices?

1. Do you often choose a pre-sweetened orange or fruit-flavoured drink over freshly squeezed orange juice?
2. Do you often eat items like processed meat pies, crisps and soft drinks?
3. Can you count on one hand the number of green vegetables (not including iceberg lettuce) that you eat in a week?
4. Do you ignore labels before you buy foods?
5. Is most of the fruit you eat canned?
6. Do you have fewer than five fruits or vegetables in your kitchen right now?
7. Do you eat just pasta on most nights?
8. Do you skip breakfast?
9. Is your daily menu very predictable?
10. Have you eaten fewer than five of the following *fresh* fruits and vegetables in the past week: spinach, papaya, melon, sweet potatoes, broccoli, asparagus, aubergine, cabbage, grapes, corn on the cob, orange, kiwi?
11. Has it been more than a week since you last ate a dark green leafy vegetable like spinach or greens?
12. Do you drink mostly tea, coffee or colas each day?
13. Have you gone on more than four rigid diets in the past three years?

14. Do you often feel like you have no energy?
15. Do you drink more than two units of alcohol daily or do you frequently go on alcohol binges and drink all night?
16. Do you smoke?
17. Do you usually choose chocolate over fruit for a snack?
18. Do you exhibit any of the following symptoms on a regular basis?
    - bruising easily
    - overwhelming fatigue
    - pale face
    - slow healing of cuts and wounds
    - weak nails and hair
    - bloodshot or cloudy eyes
    - frequent spots
19. Do you experience intense cravings for sweet or salty foods?
20. Do you feel like you could improve what you eat?

If you answered 'yes' to more than three of these questions, it could be a sign that your current diet is not providing you with an adequate variety of the necessary nutrients. You should aim for a healthy diet by following the recommendations in this book.

SMART EATING TECHNIQUES

It's unrealistic to think that you're not going to eat a bit of junk food. The key is to do it wisely so that you can eat without gaining weight, or without compromising your nutrient intake. Once you see food as life-giving fuel which should be an integral part of your lifestyle, you can start practising smart eating techniques so that you can indulge when you want to, but maintain an overall healthy diet.

Have you ever eaten a big greasy meal and then felt sick afterwards? Have you ever stuffed your face with a load of fattening things and, even though you enjoyed it at the time, later felt bloated and lethargic? Have you ever gone into a sugar coma where you fall into a heavy sleep after eating lots of sweets?

The nice thing about eating healthy foods is that, on their own, it's very difficult to eat too much. They have so much fibre and water in them – whether it's fruit, vegetables, beans or grains – that you feel extremely full long before you get to the point where you've stuffed yourself sick. And you feel much better after eating them – they rejuvenate you. It's almost impossible to feel bad, or sick, or sluggish after a nutrient-rich, fresh meal. And you omit the psychological guilt too.

But you can still have your cake, because if you eat lots of healthy food which satisfies your body's nutritional requirements, you can also eat more 'dead foods' without harming your health or contributing to a nutrient deficiency. You'll be less hungry for the dead foods, so you'll automatically eat less of them. You won't experience the desperate impulses for junk food that you had in the past because you're not starving; you're feeding yourself what your body needs on a regular schedule. So if you want chocolate too, that's fine.

The way you eat makes a difference. You can boost your calorie-burning potential, aid the digestive process, and make it easier to eat well by perfecting your eating technique. Here are some tips to incorporate into your life.

Food Preparation

- Stopping yourself from buying dead foods is the first step to eating less of them. The most nutrient-rich foods are inevitably in their most natural or raw state. When you go to the grocery store, spend most of your time in the fresh produce section, linger in the bread, beans, pulses and pasta section and make a quick stop in the dairy/meat section.
- Go for fresh or frozen, not canned fruits or vegetables.
- Eat grains in their original form: brown rice, whole wheat grains, oats/oatmeal, etc. instead of pasta, bread and breakfast cereals. Although these are carbohydrate-rich foods, they are also highly processed. The grains have been stripped of their original husks,

and have lost many nutrients in the process. Often, as is the case with some breads and most breakfast cereals, some missing nutrients are added back in, but often much of the natural fibre is lost.

- Rather than stocking up on biscuits, candy and sweets for snacks, stock up on fruit and low-fat items. At least that way you'll have to make an extra effort to eat junk and, by making a special trip to the shops, you'll burn a few extra calories in doing so.

- Keep long-lasting items like beans, grains, potatoes, pasta and low-fat crackers always on hand, as well as vegetable or chicken stock cubes, soy sauce, mustard, garlic, onions, herbs and spices.

- When you return home, wash and prepare your fruits and vegetables immediately. Fill a big bowl with water and rinse everything at once. That way, when it's time to cook, you'll have one less thing to do.

- Normally you might prepare and cook your meal, eat, then clean up the kitchen and the dishes. Since the grains and beans you'll be eating will make the food preparation time slightly longer, take those extra minutes to clean up what you can – pots you've already used, ingredients you no longer need. As something cooks (a vegetable, pasta, etc.), clean the plate or pan immediately so you don't have a daunting pile of dirty dishes to contend with after dinner. Make sure to cook your grains and beans with enough water so that the pot doesn't burn, making washing up faster.

- Aim for bright colours on your plate; when you cook, choose a healthy array of green, red, orange and yellow – all natural colourings, of course. This will ensure that the foods you are eating are supplying a wide variety of vitamins, minerals and other substances.

Retraining Your Palate

- Appreciate the taste of everything you eat. All fruits, vegetables, beans and grains have their own subtle flavour. You don't have to smother everything with creamy sauce or butter. Use a little lemon juice, pepper or salt, and experiment with herbs and spices.
- Salt isn't as bad for you as reputation has it, unless you have heart disease or osteoporosis. So feel free to use salt in moderation and other spices to enhance the flavour of your vegetables, beans and grains.

Eating Habits

- Eat foods higher in fat earlier in the day, rather than late at night.
- If you've had a stressful day, resist the inclination to 'treat' yourself with alcohol and an unhealthy convenience food. If your body is that stressed, feed it the nutrient-rich food it needs *first* to satisfy your hunger. Then, if you still need to, have a drink or snack.
- Eat frequent, smaller meals to make it easier for your body to digest the food you've eaten. Since digestion uses up energy, you'll burn more calories by digesting more frequently.
- Eat small meals more often to prevent the full, bloated feeling you get after eating large meals.
- Never let yourself get ravenously hungry. Snack and nibble – choosing healthy foods – frequently.
- Eat often to avoid hunger, even if it's just something light. If you let yourself wait too long between eating,

you're more likely to eat too much the next time you do eat.

- No matter how busy you are, do not skip lunch or breakfast.
- Do not stand or lie down when you eat. This will impair your digestive process. Sit up straight so that the digestive tract is properly aligned.
- Eat slowly. Put your fork down between bites. If you want more, you can have more, but there's no need to hurry through your meal. Chew your food over and over again. This kickstarts the digestive process and makes it easier for the nutrients to be absorbed.
- If you are in a hurry, choose a less fattening item to snack on like fruit or vegetables. Save your high-calorie foods for the meal when you can eat them and enjoy them slowly.
- Eat more here, less there. Balance what you really want with what you're not bothered about. That way you can keep the yummy fats on or in foods where it matters to you, but then you can completely cut them out in areas where you really won't notice. Some examples:
  - Skip the butter on a sandwich but keep the cheese and always use grated cheese; it takes up more space on your food, but uses less cheese than if you were to cut it in slices.
  - Go for skimmed milk and low-fat cottage cheese, but stay with semi-skimmed or regular fat milk in your tea or coffee if the taste makes a difference to you.
  - If you're having a drink on a night out when you are not bothered about the social high, skip the 150+ calories per drink and drink pure clean mineral water instead.
  - When eating pizza, skip the most fattening top-

pings, such as olives and pepperoni, and ask for sliced tomatoes, peppers, mushrooms and artichoke hearts, and even less cheese.

- Rather than having some vegetables with your pasta, have some pasta with your vegetables. Aim for 20 per cent pasta, 80 per cent vegetables, rather than the other way around.

What You Eat

- Limit, but do not cut out entirely, the amount of fat you eat. Snack on fruit, not chocolate, if possible.
- Choose fats wisely. Some fats are healthier than others. Fats and oils are made up of a mixture of 'fatty acids'. The fatty acid molecules are grouped according to their chemical structure of carbon, hydrogen and oxygen. Fatty acids with more hydrogen are said to be saturated. Oils and fats contain differing ratios of saturated and unsaturated fatty acids. When more than one-third of the fatty acids in an oil are saturated, the oil is considered to be saturated.

Since hydrogen molecules make the structure of fat more dense, saturated fats tend to be more solid. Most animal fats, including butter and lard, are saturated, as are palm and coconut oil (found in many processed foods). This kind of fat should be eaten sparingly since it is linked with high blood cholesterol levels and an increased risk of heart disease. Unsaturated fats tend to be more liquid. There are two types: monounsaturated (e.g. olive and canola oils) and polyunsaturated (e.g. corn and safflower oil). Although too much oil can still increase cholesterol and weight, these oils are healthier, especially mono-unsaturated oils which have been shown to increase good cholesterol levels.

Oils and fats also contain linoleic acid, a substance which has been shown to lower 'bad' cholesterol and triglycerides, different types of fat in the blood, while increasing 'good' cholesterol levels. Inadequate amounts of linoleic acid will result in dry or scaly skin. Oils which contain a high percentage of unsaturated fats are the healthiest and have the highest proportion of linoleic acid. Nutritionists recommend that you get 10–30 per cent of your daily calories from fat, preferably from monounsaturated oils such as olive oil and canola oil instead of butter, lard or animal fats, or from foods like avocados and nuts, that are high in fat, but have more nutrients and healthful properties than sweets and desserts.

- Choose nutrient-rich foods whenever possible.
- Choose fresh vegetables, fruit, beans and grains over all other foods. These will not only supply the nutrients you need, but they are also filled with natural fibre which will aid in the elimination of waste products from your body.
- Add a few extra vegetables to *everything* you eat, whether it is soup, salad, sandwiches, pasta, hamburgers, baked potatoes, pizza, stir fries or casseroles.

Eating Out

- Ask for oils, dressings and butter on the side. That way you can determine how much goes on your food.
- Look at the side orders and always order an extra

serving or two of fresh vegetables, so that no matter what you order, you're complementing your nutrient intake with even more healthy food.

- Bring a bagged lunch to work for more variety.
- Always include a salad that contains dark green lettuces or spinach, as well as other vegetables, to complement your meal. If you have your eye on another dish for your starter, order the salad anyway (dressing on the side). You won't add many more calories to your meal but will stock up on fibre, iron and B vitamins.
- Limit how often you reach for the bread basket. If you need to nibble, order an extra tomato or green salad (dressing on the side).
- When ordering Indian or Chinese food, request less oil or sauce in the foods.

Lazy Eating

- Always keep vegetables washed, and extra portions of brown rice or other grains and beans in the refrigerator for those times when you are too lazy to cook and it would be too easy to eat processed, ready-made dead food.
- If you're hungry and lazy and a chocolate bar is the easiest option, try eating a piece of fruit, a rice cake and other healthy fillers to see if you can quench your appetite first with something nutritious, then eat half the chocolate bar if you are still hungry.
- If you are ordering a delivery or takeaway meal, make smart choices. Ask for reduced oil on Indian and Chinese food, or create a healthier pizza.

Food Cravings

Your body will develop food cravings when several hours have passed without eating. In order to prevent a severe drop in blood sugar levels, your body will crave food that will quickly supply sugar. This is usually something fattening and sweet with very few nutrients, like chocolate, biscuits or cake, although sometimes it is for a combination of fat and sugar.

Consider your craving before acting on it. A craving isn't necessarily a bad thing. It's an indicator of either your physical or emotional state. If you haven't eaten for a while, it's a sign that your body needs food. If you are overwhelmed with emotion or stress, eating is often a way of quashing the feelings you don't want to confront. Recognise what lies beneath your craving and act accordingly. Eat wisely when satisfying a craving:

- Learn to crave healthy things by eating more of them. Experiment with different types of apples, or different ways to cook a certain vegetable.
- Don't waste time trying to talk yourself out of something fattening if you really, really want it. Eat a healthy piece of fruit first, to reduce the extent of your hunger. Then indulge, but try to reduce the portion of the fattening food if you can.
- If you're going to succumb, you might as well enjoy it. Rather than shove the whole bag of crisps in your mouth, barely leaving time to swallow, savour each bite and appreciate the taste. Take longer to eat and you'll probably be satisfied with less.
- Vary your diet. If you are getting enough of all the nutrients you need, your body will signal that it's time to eat so that you can absorb those nutrients. Most often, you don't feed your body what it needs, but

what is easiest to eat. Make sure you eat more of all the nutrient-rich foods, and you'll probably find that your cravings diminish.

- Sometimes a craving can be satisfied by a taste of what you want. You don't always have to eat the whole thing, so stop if you are no longer hungry, though this will require a great deal of self-discipline!

- Dieting makes you crave things because you are put in the psychological position of denying yourself, and everybody wants what they can't have. Free yourself from guilt by indulging. Just make sure that most of what you eat is healthy, nourishing and life-giving. The occasional extras will balance out in the long run.

- In women, hormone levels may affect cravings. If you regularly find that you eat more before your period, learn to compensate by exercising a bit more during this time.

Drink Water

It's easy to drink only coffee, tea, alcohol and cola. The caffeine in these drinks acts as a diuretic, causing you to lose water, and so it's easy to become dehydrated. Water is necessary for the functioning of all body processes, so make sure you get enough. You can tell if you are dehydrated by the colour of your urine: if it's very yellow or dark, you need more water. Aim for completely colourless urine by drinking 1–2 litres of water a day, or more if you exercise.

Portion Sizes

The 28-day *Eat More, Weigh Less* plan outlines the number of fruits and vegetables you should try to eat each day. It can seem overwhelming to try to eat 5 vegetables, 5 portions of fruit and up to 11 grain servings. But portion sizes are smaller than you think.

Learn the following servings sizes so that you can easily measure the smaller portions and larger healthy portions.

Chart 4:
Portion Sizes Made Easy

One Serving		Resembles
½ cup broccoli	=	½ tin baked beans
1 oz cheese	=	2 dominoes or a large marble or thumb size
½ cup of rice	=	1 teacup
1 serving of beans	=	2 cassette tapes stacked
1 serving of meat	=	1 deck of cards or a cassette tape
½ cup cooked pasta	=	1 tennis ball
1 cup fruit	=	a fist size

Eating More For Ever

Rather than getting stuck in a binge–purge cycle, of dieting then breaking the diet, aim to consistently eat better for the rest of your life. If you have an indulgent day, or even week, compensate by exercising a bit more and aim to balance your food choices more appropriately afterwards. Think of the nutrients in fresh food.

GETTING THE EXERCISE RIGHT

Exercise is your best weapon. Ultimately, the more you exercise, the more you can eat. When exercise is a natural part of your everyday routine, your body and mind will feel a thousand times better for it.

Of course, like eating, you don't want to become obsessed by it. Nor do you want it to interfere with your lifestyle. The key to becoming more active is to do so gradually and to make it easy and enjoyable. Eating well is a major factor because when you are well fed, you'll have the energy and inclination to exercise.

The 28-day *Eat More, Weigh Less* plan will speed up your metabolism by incorporating many types of activity into your day. When you are following the plan, and afterwards, when you have integrated the principles into your life, you'll be able to counteract food indulgences if you keep up the exercise.

But the way you exercise is crucial. You may have exercised in the past and found it didn't work. This may simply have been because you were not doing the right type of exercise. For the best results you need to burn extra calories every day by being more active and you need to do metabolism-boosting resistance exercises.

Calorie-Burning

Your general activity can be as intensive as running regularly or going to aerobics every night. Or it can require as little effort as climbing the stairs, doing more errands, getting off one stop earlier from the bus and walking – just being more active throughout the day. Ideally you want to do a combination of both. In my book *Curves – The Body Transformation Strategy*, I help you figure out how to design a personalised programme that will fit you perfectly. When you follow the 28-day plan in this book, experiment with different kinds of activity so that you find those that suit you best.

If you are short of time (or motivation), you need to get the most you can from each session. You may have heard that some types of exercise burn more fat than others. Although for many years, experts have been advocating low-intensity aerobic exercise for maximum fat-burning, new studies have proven that this is not the best way to burn calories. It's better to do *intensity training*. That is, push yourself a little harder for a shorter amount of time. You can increase the intensity slightly during the entire exercise period, or you can do short intervals where you speed yourself up for a few minutes, then lower the intensity for a few minutes, then push yourself harder again. This doesn't mean you should push yourself so hard that you are in agony. That would defeat the purpose because you would then want (and need) to stop exercising. It simply means that if you are going to devote some of your precious time to an exercise session, you need to maximise the calories you burn. Most people are not able to commit to long exercise sessions, so rather than waste your time and prolong the fat-burning process, be productive and use up a few more calories than you normally would. How much fat you burn is determined by how many calories you burn.

| the more energetic you are → the more calories you use → the more fat you burn → the more fat you lose |

Several benefits result from exercising this way:

1. You get fitter faster. So what might seem challenging at first, gets easier very quickly.

2. By exercising slightly harder, you'll not only burn more calories *during* your exercise session, you'll increase your metabolism over the 24 hours *after* you work out.

3. Some research has shown that pushing yourself in intervals during your session may suppress the absorption of new calories, forcing your body to use the fat already stored in your legs, stomach and arms for energy.

How do you do it, exactly? Instead of walking slowly for 20 minutes, you should alternate the intensity of your walk by pushing yourself to walk faster, or even do a light jog, for 3–5 minutes, then slow down to recover for another five minutes, and then continue to alternate the intensities. As you get fitter, you'll be able to work at higher intensities for longer, but it won't seem harder because you'll be in shape.

This way you maximise your exercise time. You'll burn the most calories you can during that period. This also means you can shorten your exercise time if necessary: instead of doing a slow 45-minute walk, you can do a faster 25-minute higher-intensity walk.

You can apply intensity training to any type of aerobic exercise you do. When you follow the activity pro- gramme in the 28-day *Eat More, Weigh Less* plan, make sure to apply intensity training to your workout.

Lift Weight to Lose Weight

Since aerobic exercise does not target specific muscles to build strength (and therefore more muscle mass), it doesn't have much of a long-term effect on your meta- bolism. So in addition to using up more energy by moving more, you will also need to do a little bit of muscle strengthening each week. These exercises are best performed with weights. You'll do less in a shorter amount of time, and they'll be more effective at repla- cing your lost muscle. You can permanently raise your metabolism by increasing the amount of muscle in your body. This means you'll burn more calories *all day and all night* – while you eat, sleep and exercise. This will prevent you from becoming flabby, and the extra muscle you tone up will help speed up your metabolism, so that in the long run, you can eat more without gaining weight.

Resistance training – exercises with weights or bands – is the most effective way to build muscle mass. But don't worry about bulking up. At this stage you're simply trying to maintain what you're losing as you age and become more inactive.

In the 28-day *Eat More, Weigh Less* plan I give you a set of exercises to do each week which incorporate resistance training. These are slow exercises which will work all your major body parts. Since these moves are very precise, it's important to get the technique right. In my book *The Squeeze*, I take an in-depth look at how to reshape your body by using weights and give you pointers on alignment and how to focus on the appropriate muscle. By lifting weights and doing cardiovascular exercise just 2–3 times a week, you'll decrease body fat and tone your flabby bits. You'll not only function better, you'll feel and look years younger too!

Chart 5:
Metabolism-Boosting Exercise Technique

1. Move slowly. The quicker you go, the more you rely on momentum, not muscular control.
2. Straighten your elbows and knees without locking them.
3. Pay attention to strain. If you feel fatigue in the middle of a muscle, this is a sign that you are stimulating the muscle appropriately. If you feel pain in a joint, it's a sign that you have pushed yourself too far or have poor alignment.
4. Do resistance exercises no more than 2–3 times a week – every other day. This gives the muscle fibres a chance to rest and become stronger.
5. Breathe throughout the movement. Ideally you should exhale with the effort (when you are moving the weight with force), and inhale during the return phase of the exercise.
6. Vary the amount of weight you use. Some muscle groups are stronger than others. Hold two weights in one hand if you do not have a selection of different sizes.

7. Warm up and cool down before and after any exercise.
8. Perform flexibility stretches at least twice a week. Try to hold each stretch for 10–60 seconds.
9. Focus on squeezing the muscle you are working to move the weight, rather than the other way around.
10. Think quality, not quantity. After each set of 8–12 repetitions, your muscles should feel fatigued.

PART TWO

THE 28-DAY EAT MORE, WEIGH LESS PLAN

If you're ready to start looking good, feeling great and weighing *less* from eating *more*, then you're ready to start the 28-day *Eat More, Weigh Less* plan.

This plan gives you daily menus and an activity plan to follow. The plan caters for you in several ways. If you like to follow regimented diets, there is a daily menu with recipes at the back. To make your food preparation even easier, I've included a shopping list at the beginning of each week, highlighting the key items you'll need to follow the plan exactly.

If you do not have the discipline to stick to the detailed menu, or if you eat out often and are unable to prepare special dishes, then you can still follow the principles of the plan. Instead of using the exact recipes or menus, arrange your daily meals to meet the eating goal. This guideline will suggest how many different servings of fruits, grains, vegetables and pulses to eat that day along with the other foods in your diet.

The activity suggestions are flexible too, and there are two levels of programme you can follow, depending upon your current fitness level.

How to Follow the Plan

Shopping list

To save your time and make the plan easier to follow, this lists most of the fresh foods you will need each week if you are following the daily menus. The list may vary according to your portion sizes and the number of people you are cooking for. Also, some items may not be to your taste, or available to you locally, so you may need to find substitutes. You should also keep a supply of the basics like beans, grains, pasta and other dry goods.

Menu

This daily plan is designed so that you can eat as often as seven or eight times a day! By eating so often you will not feel the insatiable food cravings which make you binge on bad, unnutritious foods. As well as loading up on plenty of fruits and vegetables, you will include some sweets and butter and cheese in your meals. The key is to use these sparingly, and when possible use low-fat versions.

You do not need to eat the exact items given. The menu is a guideline to show you how to eat more nutritiously for the rest of your life. Feel free to substitute the fruits and vegetables used in any of the recipes. Where specific quantities are not given (melon, strawberries, broccoli), this is because you can eat practically limitless amounts of these foods without gaining weight.

The timing of when you eat your meals is flexible, but aim to have your main meals about four or five hours apart, with light snacks in between. You do not *have* to snack at each designated time during the day, but know you can if you need to. Just make sure not to go more than 3–4 hours without some light food, or you may binge later to compensate for the energy-draining low blood sugar level and subsequent hunger you may feel.

When following the specific menu plan, try to arrange your food preparation time as quickly as possible. These meals may not be as immediate as going to McDonald's or zapping pre-made food in the microwave, but they can be nearly as fast if you plan wisely. Read the chapter on 'Smart Eating Techniques' for food preparation tips.

Chart 6:
Sample Eating Schedule

Eye-opener	8 a.m.
Breakfast	9 a.m.
Snack	11 a.m.
Lunch	1 p.m.
Snack	4 or 5 p.m.
Dinner	7 p.m.
Lite snack	10 p.m.

Eye-Opener and Energy Burst

Each morning I wake you up with a fresh dose of rejuvenating fruit. Then I give you some simple movement to do. You can either go for a brisk walk outside your house, or you can turn on the radio and boogie to a couple of songs. This is effortless exercise that does not entail going to the gym or pushing yourself too hard; it's a little bit of activity to get you moving in the morning. The Energy Burst is meant to be easy, fast and relaxed. Don't worry about putting on special exercise gear, just move. If you have an exercise bike or other piece of equipment, you can jump on that. Just do *something*. Then you can shower and dress and eat a yummy breakfast.

This Energy Burst is a vital part of your plan because not only will it help revive you on a sleepy morning and jump-start your day, but the exercise will also have a major impact on your health and weight. Studies show that even little bits of exercise will improve your health. Most importantly, exercise done *regularly* will make the most difference in maintaining or losing weight. Your commitment to longer exercise sessions will sometimes be altered by how busy your schedule gets. If you can at least maintain your easy, effortless bits of exercise you'll still help keep yourself in shape. In fact, the short 5 or 10 minutes you take each morning for these Energy Bursts will enable you to lose up to 10 pounds in the next 12 months, *without dieting*.

Daytime Activity

In addition to the short Energy Burst in the morning, I have designed a four-week fitness programme for you to follow which includes both calorie-burning and muscle-strengthening exercise. This exercise will help increase your metabolism which will in turn enable you to eat more. The *Eat More, Weigh Less* programme works because when you eat more nutritious food, you'll have more energy. Exercise won't seem like such a chore, providing you choose the appropriate activity for you and work at a reasonable pace, and you'll find it more enjoyable than you may have in the past. When you exercise regularly, you'll find you have more energy, which carries over into other areas of your life.

I have designed the programme for two levels. Choose the Level 1 plan if you have never exercised or have not done so in over six months. Choose Level 2 if you exercise sporadically.

Depending on your fitness level, you should modify the plan to suit you. If Level 1 is too much because you literally have not done any exercise for 20 years, then do less and work your way up so that you can follow the plan. You'll be amazed at how fast your body responds to exercise. Your first few days may seem tiring. After two weeks you'll see how much easier the same amount of exercise suddenly becomes.

If you are a regular exerciser and find that Level 2 is not enough, feel free to modify the length of the sessions. Beware of the trap of exercising more and more, however. If exercise takes up too much time or you push yourself too hard, you're more likely to give it up. Over the long term, the consistency of doing exercise over the period of a year is more important than whether you spent 75 minutes or 25 minutes during one particular session.

Your schedule will suggest a time period to spend on a 'fat-burning' activity, or exercise where you move your whole body and burn lots of calories. You can choose from the activities on the following list. Try to vary the activities you do.

Fat-Burning Activities

walking	swimming	tennis	running
aerobics	step aerobics	squash	cycling
inline skating	rambling	rowing	gym/aerobic machines
soccer	aqua aerobics	dancing	water running
skiing	rugby	netball	

You will also do 'metabolism-boosting' exercises which target specific body parts. A different set of exercises focusing on the main muscle groups will be given each week. You will see faster results if you use weights. Weights are safe even if you are a beginner. You can buy them at any local department or sports store. Start with 2–4 pound dumb-bells and work your way up to 5–12 pounds. You can also try out makeshift weights at home by using a tin of beans or bag of sugar in each hand. These will be much more awkward, so once you are able, buy a more user-friendly pair of dumb-bells.

If you switch the exercise days on your weekly plan, never do the 'metabolism-boosting' resistance exercises more than three times a week. Leave a day of rest in between so your muscles have time to recover properly and become stronger and firmer.

Eating Goal

Each day you will be reminded to include a good variety of fruits, vegetables, beans and grains in your diet. The 28-day *Eat More, Weigh Less* plan is based on the US Department of Agriculture food guide pyramid. Since you are trying to achieve *optimum* health and vitality, the plan veers towards the higher amounts of servings, particularly of vegetables, whole grains, beans and fruit (see p. 29). Most serving sizes are small, so it is relatively easy to obtain your requirement, provided that you eat a healthy, varied diet.

If you are not following the specific menu plan, only the guidelines, aim for as much variety as you can. Include plenty of grains and beans in your diet. Do not deprive yourself of so-called 'bad' or fattening foods. Instead, rearrange how you eat them. Since you can eat virtually limitless amounts of fruit and vegetables, be generous with those portions and put the more filling food in smaller amounts on your plate. Eat fattening foods early in the day – I've included 'Indulgences' on the menu several times a week so you can eat a chocolate bar or biscuits as well.

Chart 7:
Recommended Quality and Quantity of Daily Meals

Food type	Rec. servings per day	Sample serving size (one portion)
Whole grains	6–11 servings	½ cup rice or 1 slice bread
Vegetables	3–5 servings	1 cup raw leafy vegetables or ½ cup other vegetables or ¾ cup vegetable juice
Fruit	2–4	1 apple or 1 banana or 1 orange or ½ cup berries or ¾ cup fruit juice
Dairy	2–3	1 cup milk or 1 cup yoghurt or 1½oz cheese
Dry beans, peas, nuts, lean meat, chicken or fish	2–3	½ cup cooked beans or 2–3oz lean meat, poultry or fish

1 cup = 8oz = 240ml

Source: United States Department of Agriculture

WEEK ONE
Eat More, Weigh Less Plan

DAY 1

Shopping list

FRUIT	VEGETABLES	
1 lemon	2 stalks broccoli	Rocket
3 bananas	½lb spinach	Corn salad lettuce
1 grapefruit	2 potatoes	Mangetout
3 apples	1 sweet potato	Cabbage
4 oranges	Asparagus	Courgettes
Grapes	Fresh peas	Fresh basil
1 mango	2 corn on the cob	Cucumbers
1 pint strawberries	2 red bell peppers	Puy lentils
Melon	Carrots	Barley

Menu

Eye-Opener	Fresh-squeezed orange juice
Energy Burst	Walk or dance for 10 minutes
Breakfast	Apple/cinnamon oatmeal
Snack	Banana
Lunch	Red pepper & cheese sandwich
Snack	Strawberries
Dinner	Green pasta with broccoli, courgettes & basil; fresh corn with lime
Lite Snack	Green grapes

Activity

Level 1:	10 mins fat-burning activity
	metabolism-boosting exercises
Level 2:	20 mins fat-burning activity

Eating goal

Eat at least: 4 fresh vegetables, 2 fresh pieces of fruit, 1 serving of beans

DAY 2

Menu

Eye-Opener	Fresh lemon
Energy Burst	Walk or dance for 10 minutes
Breakfast	Low-fat yoghurt with oat & barley flakes
Snack	Low-fat crackers
Lunch	Baked potato with corn
Indulgence	KitKat
Snack	Carrot & cucumbers
Dinner	Wild rice & puy lentils; broccoli with lemon, spinach & pea salad
Lite Snack	Peach

Activity

Level 1:   10 mins fat-burning activity
Level 2:   20 mins fat-burning activity
metabolism-boosting exercises

Eating goal

Eat at least: 3 fresh pieces of fruit, 3 fresh vegetables, 2 different grains

DAY 3

Menu

Eye-Opener	Fresh-squeezed carrot juice
Energy Burst	Walk or dance for 5 minutes
Breakfast	Wholegrain bagel with lite cream cheese
Snack	Apple
Lunch	Vegetable soup, green salad
Snack	Baked crisps
Dinner	Spiced rice, spinach & roasted red peppers, four-bean salad
Lite Snack	Carrot sticks

Activity

Level 1:	15 mins fat-burning activity
Level 2:	15 mins fat-burning activity
	metabolism-boosting exercises

Eating goal

Eat at least: 3 fresh vegetables, 2 pieces of fruit, 1 serving of beans and 1 wholegrain

DAY 4

Menu

Eye-Opener	Fresh papaya
Energy Burst	Walk or dance for 5 minutes
Breakfast	Tropical cottage cheese
Snack	Fat-free popcorn
Lunch	Baked potato with beans and corn
Indulgence	2 scoops ice-cream
Snack	Rice cakes
Dinner	Broccoli & barley soup, almost raw vegetable salad, lemon potatoes
Lite Snack	Apple

Activity

Level 1:	15 mins fat-burning activity
	metabolism-boosting exercises
Level 2:	25 mins fat-burning activity

Eating goal

Eat at least: 3 fresh pieces of fruit, 4 fresh vegetables, 1 serving of a grain and beans

DAY 5

Eye-Opener	Fresh-squeezed grapefruit juice
Energy Burst	Walk or dance for 5 minutes
Breakfast	Banana oatmeal
Snack	Carrots and celery
Lunch	Tomato, cucumber & cheese on granary bread
Snack	Airpopped popcorn
Dinner	Tomato, basil & rice noodles, minestrone soup, steamed broccoli
Lite Snack	Strawberries

Activity

| Level 1: | Have a rest-day! |
| Level 2: | metabolism-boosting exercises |

Eating goal

Eat: 5 pieces of fresh fruit, 4 vegetables, 1 wholegrain

DAY 6

Menu

Eye-Opener	Fresh strawberries
Energy Burst	Walk or dance for 10 minutes
Breakfast	Homemade muesli with skimmed milk
Snack	Banana & strawberry smoothie
Lunch	Broccoli soup, rice & vegetables
Indulgence	4 chocolate chip cookies
Snack	Carrot sticks
Dinner	Tiny pizza with red pepper, spinach & mushrooms, rocket & asparagus salad
Lite Snack	Orange

Activity

Level 1:   15 mins fat-burning activity
Level 2:   25 mins fat-burning activity

Eating goal

Eat at least: 4 fresh vegetables, 3 pieces of fruit, 1 serving of beans

DAY 7

Eye-Opener	Fresh cherries and grapes
Energy Burst	Walk or dance for 10 minutes
Breakfast	Fruit with fromage frais
Snack	Tomatoes & cucumber with lemon
Lunch	Baked chips, green salad, chunky vegetable soup
Snack	Sliced sweet red peppers
Dinner	Black-eyed bean bake, crunchy slaw, steamed mangetout & carrots
Lite Snack	Orange

Activity

Level 1:	15 mins fat-burning activity metabolism-boosting exercises
Level 2:	30 mins fat-burning activity metabolism-boosting exercises

Eating goal

Eat at least: 5 fresh vegetables, 4 pieces of fresh fruit, 1 wholegrain

WEEK ONE
Metabolism-Boosting Exercises

The following exercises will stretch and sculpt your major muscles. Do these 2–3 times a week according to the plan. Move slowly to control each movement. You'll see faster results if you use weights. Start with 2–3lb and work up to 5–10lb. Vary your weights, as some muscles may be stronger than others.

Torso and Inner Thigh Stretch

Stand in a wide straddle position. Bend your knees and lower your hips. Rest your left hand on your thigh. Reach your right arm above your head. Rather than bending sideways, lift your ribs and lengthen your spine. Hold for 10–15 seconds, then switch sides.

SAFETY TIP: Avoid bouncing. Hold still while you stretch.

Thigh and Calf Stretch

Stand with your left leg in front of you. With a straight back, lean your body forward and rest your left hand on your left thigh. Press your hips back to feel the stretch in the back of your front leg. Then gently raise your front toe. Hold for 15–20 seconds, then switch sides.

SAFETY TIP: If the stretch in the back of your legs feels too tight, bend your front knee slightly and drop your front toe.

Hip and Thigh Stretch

Stand with your right leg in front and your left leg behind your body. Point both toes forward. Bend your knees and lower your hips slightly. Press your left hip forwards. Hold for 5–15 seconds, then switch legs.

SAFETY TIP: If you feel pain in your back knee then straighten your left leg more.

Bum and Thigh Tightener

a. Stand with your feet shoulder width apart, both toes pointing forward. Hold weights in each hand by each side. With a straight back, lean forward at a diagonal. Push your hips out behind you and lower until you reach knee level. Keep your body weight in your heels, not toes. Pull your bellybutton in to support your lower back.

b. Squeeze your buttocks and straighten your legs to standing as you bend your elbows and bring your hands to your shoulders. Lower slowly. Do two sets of 12.

SAFETY TIP: If your knees feel strained, make sure you push your hips out so that your calves stay vertical, not slanted, when your knees are bent.

Shoulder Shaper

Stand with your legs wide apart, knees slightly bent. With weights in each hand, place your arms by your sides, palms in. As you exhale, tighten your shoulders and raise both arms to horizontal. Keep your ribs lifted. Hold then slowly lower. Do two sets of 12.

SAFETY TIP: To avoid excess stress, do not lift your hands higher than shoulder level.

Waist Firmer

a. Stand with your right leg bent in front, both toes pointing forward. Rest your right hand on your right thigh, then lean forward with a straight back. Hold the weight in your left hand and let it hang to the floor.

b. As you exhale, pull your left elbow to your ribcage. As you raise your arm, open your chest to the left side and pull your left shoulder back. Do two sets of 12, then switch sides.

SAFETY TIP: To protect the lower back, make sure your body weight is supported by leaning into your front thigh.

Midriff Sculptor

Lie on your back, knees bent, feet flat. Hold a dumb-bell behind your head, and keep your chin off your chest. Pull your bellybutton in to flatten your lower abdominals. Lift your shoulder blades off the ground. From this starting position, exhale and move your ribcage towards your hips. Hold at the top then lower just to your shoulder blades. Do two sets of 12 slowly.

SAFETY TIP: If your neck hurts, avoid pulling on your head. Rest your head in your hands like a pillow.

Upper Arm Toner

a. Stand with your feet shoulder width apart. With a straight back lean forward at a diagonal. Hold your bellybutton in to support your lower back. Hold a weight in each hand, bend your elbows and pull them back past your ribcage.

b. As you exhale, tighten the back of your upper arms and straighten your elbows. Hold, then bend your elbows, keeping your upper arm lifted. Only the lower arms move during this exercise. Do two sets of 12.

SAFETY TIP: If your lower back feels strained, work one arm at a time and rest the other hand on your thigh for support.

Inner Thigh and Upper Back Strengthener

Stand with your feet wide apart, toes turned out. Bend your knees and lower your hips. Hold your weights overhead. Lift your right heel off the ground and press your body weight into your right toe. Squeeze your buttocks and drag your right foot to the left, straightening your legs to standing as you do so. At the same time, lower your hands to your shoulders. Hold, lower into a wide squat again,
straighten your arms to the ceiling and repeat on the other side. Do two sets of 15.

SAFETY TIP: If your knees feel strained push your hips out behind your back when your knees are bent so your weight stays on your heels, not toes.

Waist Twist

Lie on your back, knees bent, feet flat. Hold a dumb-bell on your right shoulder. Place your left hand behind your head. Pull your bellybutton in to flatten the lower abdomen, then lift your shoulder blades off the ground. As you exhale, push your right shoulder to the left to rotate the ribcage. Hold, then slowly untwist. Do two sets of 12, then switch sides.

SAFETY TIP: Keep your pelvis stable as your torso twists.

Abdominal Flattener

a. Support yourself on your hand and knees. Hold your back completely straight. Pull your bellybutton into your spine without moving your pelvis or back. Tighten the lower abdominal area in between your hips.

b. Raise your left leg slowly. Tighten your lower abdominal muscles to stabilise your pelvis as you move your hips. Lower your leg slowly, then switch legs. Do eight on each side slowly.

SAFETY TIP: If this is uncomfortable on your knees, rest on a towel or mat.

WEEK TWO
Eat More, Weigh Less Plan

DAY 8

Shopping list

FRUIT	VEGETABLES	
Melon	2 stalks broccoli	Courgettes
3 bananas	½lb spinach	Mangetout
1 papaya	2 potatoes	French beans
1 grapefruit	1 sweet potato	Mushrooms
3 apples	Asparagus	Artichokes
4 oranges	Red & yellow peppers	Celery
1 mango	Rocket	Brown rice
1 pint strawberries	Okra	Lentils
Cherries	Tomatoes	Butterbeans
Peach	Celery	Barley
Grapes	Watercress	Black beans
Nectarine	Corn	

Menu

Eye-Opener	Fresh melon
Energy Burst	Walk or dance for 5 minutes
Breakfast	Rye toast & a soft-boiled egg
Snack	Banana
Lunch	Tomato soup, green salad
Snack	Sliced sweet red pepper
Dinner	Rocket & lentil soup, Provençal salad, okra & tomatoes
Lite Snack	Orange

Activity

Level 1:	20 mins fat-burning activity
Level 2:	25 mins fat-burning activity

Eating goal

Eat at least: 5 fresh pieces of fruit, 3 fresh vegetables, 2 different grains

DAY 9

Menu

Eye-Opener	Fresh papaya
Energy Burst	Walk or dance for 10 minutes
Breakfast	Apple cinnamon oatmeal
Snack	Carrot & celery
Lunch	Baked potato with beans
Snack	Airpopped popcorn
Dinner	Cappellini with raw tomato & basil, yellow squash & carrots, rocket & red pepper salad
Lite Snack	Green grapes

Activity

Level 1:	15 mins fat-burning activity metabolism-boosting exercises
Level 2:	30 mins fat-burning activity metabolism-boosting exercises

Eating goal

Eat at least: 3 fresh pieces of fruit, at least 4 fresh vegetables and 1 wholegrain

DAY 10

Eye-Opener	Fresh squeezed orange juice
Energy Burst	Walk or dance for 10 minutes
Breakfast	Juicy fruit with cottage cheese
Snack	Fat-free baked crisps
Lunch	Rye sandwich with red pepper/cheese
Snack	Apple
Dinner	Broccoli, watercress & barley soup, Greek spinach salad, butterbeans & new potatoes
Lite Snack	Carrot sticks

Activity

Level 1:	20 mins fat-burning activity
Level 2:	30 mins fat-burning activity

Eating goal

Eat at least: 5 fresh vegetables, 3 fresh pieces of fruit, 1 serving of beans and 1 wholegrain

DAY 11

Eye-Opener	Fresh strawberries
Energy Burst	Walk or dance for 5 minutes
Breakfast	Low-fat yoghurt with oat & barley flakes
Snack	Tomatoes & cucumbers with lemon
Lunch	Wholewheat sandwich with cheese and salad
Indulgence	2 scoops ice-cream
Snack	Carrot sticks
Dinner	Spiced rice and black beans, chunky vegetable soup, steamed okra & asparagus
Lite Snack	Apple

Activity

Level 1:	Have a rest day!
Level 2:	Have a rest day!

Eating goal

Eat at least: 3 fresh pieces of fruit, at least 4 fresh vegetables, 1 serving of beans

DAY 12

Eye-Opener	Fresh-squeezed carrot juice
Energy Burst	Walk or dance for 5 minutes
Breakfast	Fruit with fromage frais
Snack	Fat-free popcorn
Lunch	Baked potato with corn
Snack	Sliced sweet red pepper
Dinner	Spicy sesame rice noodles, oriental broccoli & mangetout, green & yellow salad
Lite Snack	Nectarine

Activity

Level 1:	20 mins fat-burning activity metabolism-boosting exercises
Level 2:	25 mins fat-burning activity metabolism-boosting exercises

Eating goal

Eat at least: 5 fresh pieces of fruit, 4 vegetables, 1 wholegrain and 1 serving of beans

DAY 13

Menu

Eye-Opener	Fresh cherries and grapes
Energy Burst	Walk or dance for 10 minutes
Breakfast	Wholegrain bagel, lite cream cheese
Snack	Peach and banana smoothie
Lunch	Vegetable soup, green salad
Snack	Rice cakes
Dinner	Red pepper couscous, 3-bean soup, fresh corn with lime
Lite Snack	Orange

Activity

Level 1:	20 mins fat-burning activity
Level 2:	35 mins fat-burning activity

Eating goal

Eat at least: 3 fresh vegetables, 3 fresh pieces of fruit, 1 serving of beans

DAY 14

Eye-Opener	Fresh grapefruit juice
Energy Burst	Walk or dance for 10 minutes
Breakfast	Homemade muesli with skimmed milk
Snack	Fat-free crackers with low-fat cheese
Indulgence	Chocolate bar
Lunch	Baked chips, steamed broccoli
Snack	Banana
Dinner	Blackeyed bean bake, tomatoes with basil, asparagus & courgettes
Lite Snack	Carrot sticks

Activity

Level 1:	15 mins fat-burning activity metabolism-boosting exercises
Level 2:	25 mins fat-burning activity metabolism-boosting exercises

Eating goal

Eat at least: 4 fresh vegetables, 4 pieces of fresh fruit, 1 serving of beans

WEEK TWO
Metabolism-Boosting Exercises

The following exercises will stretch and sculpt your major muscles. Do these 2–3 times a week according to the plan. Move slowly to control each movement. You'll see faster results if you use weights. Start with 2–3lb and work up to 5–10lb. Vary your weights, as some muscles may be stronger than others.

Back, Waist and Thigh Stretch

Sit with right leg extended and left leg bent so the left foot rests inside of the straight knee. Hold your ribs high as you raise your left arm to the ceiling. Rotate your chest out and lengthen your spine. Hold for 10 seconds, then switch sides.

SAFETY TIP: To support your spine, rest your body weight on your right hand.

Back Thigh Lengthener

Lie on your back with your left knee bent. Extend your right leg to the ceiling holding on to the back of your thigh. Keep your knee slightly bent. As you exhale, push your heel higher. Hold for 5–20 seconds then switch sides.

SAFETY TIP: If you feel strain in your calf, point your toe.

Hip Relaxer

Lie on your back and bend both thighs into your chest. Place one hand on each knee and circle your legs in opposing directions four times. Reverse directions.

SAFETY TIP: Keep your legs close to your body.

Buttocks Stretch

Lie on your back with your knees bent, feet flat. Cross your right leg over your left, then bring your left thigh to your chest. Hold for 15 seconds, then switch sides.

SAFETY TIP: If your knee hurts, straighten your top leg slightly so your knee does not twist.

Upper Arm Curl

a. Stand slightly staggered, right foot in front of the left. Hold a weight in each hand. To start, straighten your right arm and drop in front of your right thigh. At the same time straighten your left arm behind you so that your hand points behind you, palm facing in. Then bend your left elbow – keep it lifted and close to your ribs.

b. As you exhale, bring your right hand to your right shoulder, and straighten your left arm without dropping the elbow. Return to starting position. Do two sets of 12, then switch sides.

   SAFETY TIP: Keep your back straight, shoulders pulled back.

Upper Back Straightener

a. Stand with your right leg on a step or stool. Press your chest forward and lean on your front thigh. Hold a weight in each hand and reach your arms out in front. Pull your bellybutton in to support your lower back.

b. As you exhale, raise your elbows out to the side and up to the ceiling, letting your hands hang down. Feel your shoulder blades pull together as your elbows point up. Inhale as you slowly lower the arms. Do two sets of 12.

   SAFETY TIP: If your lower back feels strained, lift your ribs to lengthen the spine.

Leg and Buttock Tightener

Stand with your feet shoulder width apart, both toes pointing out. Hold your weights on your hips. With a straight back, lean forward at a diagonal. Hold your lower abdomen tight. Push back as you lower your hips to knee level. Squeeze your buttocks and inner thighs to straighten up again. Do two sets of 15.

SAFETY TIP: To avoid straining your knees, keep your body weight on your heels, not toes.

Back and Buttock Strengthener

a. Stand with your feet parallel, knees slightly bent. Hold a weight in your right hand in front of your thigh, palm down. Contract your lower abdomen.

b. As you exhale, lean slightly forward as you raise your left leg behind and right hand in front until your arm and leg form a diagonal line. Lower your arm and leg. Do two sets of eight repetitions, then switch sides.

SAFETY TIP: Keep your chin down so your neck stays aligned with your spine.

Posture Perfector

Practise perfect standing to develop strength in your postural muscles. Lengthen your spine and imagine yourself standing taller. Hold your shoulders down and slightly back. Lift your ribs and flatten your abdomen. Balance your heels and mid-foot. Relax your pelvis and keep your knees soft.

   SAFETY TIP: Correct your posture throughout the day (in a queue, when you are cooking, talking on the phone, etc.) by holding yourself in this position.

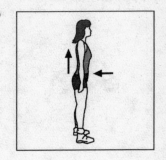

Chest, Back and Shoulder Lift

a. Stand with your left leg in front. Lean forward with a straight back and rest your left hand on your thigh. Move your right hand (holding a weight) across your chest to the left side.

b. As you exhale, tighten the back of your shoulders and open your right arm to shoulder level. Slowly lower. Do two sets of 12. Then switch sides.
   SAFETY TIP: Avoid rounding your spine. Press your chest forward.

Abdominal Toner

Lie on your back with your knees bent. Hold a weight on your chest, with the other hand supporting your head. Exhale while you pull your bellybutton in, then move your ribs to your hips. Hold and pull your bellybutton in more. Then bring your ribs farther forward. Inhale as you slowly lower. Do 15 slowly.

SAFETY TIP: Avoid pulling your head. Concentrate on squeezing your abs.

Waist Shaper

Lie on your back, knees bent. Place your left hand behind your head and hold a weight in your right hand above your chest. Straighten your left leg. Exhale and rotate your ribs towards your left hip. Lower. Do 15. Then change sides.

SAFETY TIP: Keep your elbow straight throughout the movement.

WEEK THREE
Eat More, Weigh Less Plan

DAY 15

Shopping list

FRUIT	VEGETABLES	
1 cantaloup	2 stalks broccoli	Rocket
3 bananas	½lb spinach	Cherry tomatoes
1 grapefruit	2 potatoes	Corn
3 apples	1 sweet potato	Red beans
4 oranges	Asparagus	Barley
1 papaya	Carrots	Fava or broad beans
1 pint strawberries	Red bell peppers	Black beans
Blueberries	Tomatoes	Barley flakes
Grapes	Fresh peas	Low-fat yoghurt
1 pear	Cabbage	Couscous
1 lime	Green beans	

Menu

Eye-Opener	Fresh cantaloup
Energy Burst	Walk or dance for 10 minutes
Breakfast	Tropical cottage cheese
Snack	Fat-free baked crisps
Lunch	Wholewheat sandwich with cheese and tomato
Snack	Apple
Dinner	Red bean & barley soup, spinach & roasted red peppers, tomatoes with basil
Lite Snack	Carrot sticks

Activity

Level 1:	15 mins fat-burning activity
Level 2:	20 mins fat-burning activity

Eating goal

Eat at least: 3 fresh pieces of fruit, 4 fresh vegetables, 2 different grains

DAY 16

Eye-Opener	Fresh strawberries
Energy Burst	Walk or dance for 5 minutes
Breakfast	Banana & almond oatmeal
Snack	Rice cakes
Lunch	Baked potato with corn
Indulgence	4 chocolate chip cookies
Snack	Airpopped popcorn
Dinner	Spiced rice and fava or broad beans, Greek spinach salad, steamed broccoli and carrots
Lite Snack	Orange

Activity

Level 1:	Have a rest day!
Level 2:	25 mins fat-burning activity

Eating goal

Eat at least: 3 fresh pieces of fruit, 4 fresh vegetables, 1 wholegrain

DAY 17

Menu

Eye-Opener	Fresh papaya
Energy Burst	Walk or dance for 5 minutes
Breakfast	Rye toast and a soft-boiled egg
Snack	Banana
Lunch	Green salad, low-fat yoghurt
Snack	Baked crisps
Dinner	Carrot & pea soup, red pepper, couscous, fresh corn with lime
Lite Snack	Strawberries

Activity

Level 1:	20 mins fat-burning activity metabolism-boosting exercises
Level 2:	metabolism-boosting exercises

Eating goal

Eat at least: 4 fresh vegetables, 3 fresh pieces of fruit, 1 serving of beans and 1 wholegrain

DAY 18

Menu

Eye-Opener	Fresh-squeezed orange juice
Energy Burst	Walk or dance for 10 minutes
Breakfast	Low-fat yoghurt with oat & barley flakes
Snack	Apple
Lunch	Baked potato with beans
Indulgence	1 slice apple pie
Snack	Carrot sticks
Dinner	Brown rice and black beans, broccoli with cheese, almost raw vegetable salad
Lite Snack	Airpopped popcorn

Activity

Level 1:	15 mins fat-burning activity
Level 2:	30 mins fat-burning activity

Eating goal

Eat at least: 4 fresh pieces of fruit, 4 fresh vegetables, 1 serving of a grain and beans

DAY 19

Eye-Opener	Fresh grapes and blueberries
Energy Burst	Walk or dance for 5 minutes
Breakfast	Fruit with fromage frais
Snack	Fat-free crackers
Lunch	Rye bread with cheese and salad
Snack	Carrot & cucumbers
Dinner	Provençal salad, lemon potatoes, vegetable barley soup
Lite Snack	Orange

Activity

Level 1:	metabolism-boosting exercises
Level 2:	metabolism-boosting exercises

Eating goal

Eat: 5 fresh pieces of fruit, 1 wholegrain

DAY 20

Eye-Opener	Fresh-squeezed grapefruit juice
Energy Burst	Walk or dance for 10 minutes
Breakfast	Homemade muesli with skimmed milk
Snack	Strawberry, pear & banana smoothie
Lunch	Chunky vegetable soup with green salad
Snack	Airpopped popcorn
Dinner	Rocket gnocchi with cherry tomatoes, crunchy slaw, steamed green beans
Lite Snack	Green grapes

Activity

Level 1:	20 mins fat-burning activity
Level 2:	30 mins fat-burning activity
	metabolism-boosting exercises

Eating goal

Eat at least: 5 fresh vegetables, 3 fresh pieces of fruit, 1 serving of beans

DAY 21

Menu

Eye-Opener	Fresh-squeezed carrot juice
Energy Burst	Walk or dance for 10 minutes
Breakfast	Wholegrain bagel & lite cream cheese
Snack	Red pepper & tomato salad
Lunch	Baked chips, steamed vegetables, salad
Snack	Melon
Dinner	Tomato, cheese and vegetable bake, spinach and fresh pea salad
Lite Snack	Strawberries

Activity

Level 1:	25 mins fat-burning activity metabolism-boosting exercises
Level 2:	35 mins fat-burning activity metabolism-boosting exercises

Eating goal

Eat at least: 3 fresh vegetables, 3 fresh pieces of fruit, 1 wholegrain

WEEK THREE
Metabolism-Boosting Exercises

The following exercises will stretch and sculpt your major muscles. Do these 2–3 times a week according to the plan. Move slowly to control each movement. You'll see faster results if you use weights. Start with 2–3lb and work up to 5–10lb. Vary your weights, as some muscles may be stronger than others.

Back and Shoulder Stretch

Stand with your legs wide apart, knees bent. Rest your hands on your thighs. Lean your right shoulder towards the centre and turn your head to the left. Hold for 10 seconds, then switch sides.

SAFETY TIP: Lean your body weight into your thighs.

Neck and Lower Back Relaxer

Lie on your back and bring your knees to your chest. Hold on to the back of your legs and gently roll your head from side to side.

SAFETY TIP: Press your neck into the floor and move your head slowly.

Thigh Stretch

Sit with your legs extended. Open your feet to a comfortable V position where you feel a pleasant stretch in your inner thighs. Hold for 10–15 seconds. Keep your ribs high, then turn towards your right leg. With a straight back, lean over your thigh. Hold for 15–30 seconds until you feel the back of your thighs loosen, then switch sides.

SAFETY TIP: If you feel strain in your lower back, avoid slumping. Hold your spine tall and lean your torso weight forward. Do not bounce or attempt to get your head to your knee.

Hip and Thigh Lengthener

Stand with your right leg in front, left leg back, both toes pointing forward. Hold your spine tall. Bend both knees slightly and press your left hip forward. Hold for 15 seconds, then switch sides.

SAFETY TIP: Open your legs wide enough for your front calf to stay perpendicular, not slanted, to the floor.

Buttocks Sculptor

a. Start with your feet shoulder width apart and parallel. Hold a weight in each hand, arms by your side. Step forward as far as possible, landing with your heel first. Bend your front knee and lower your hips until your front thigh is parallel to the floor. Keep your knee over your ankle, *not* your toe.

b. Contract your buttocks and push your front heel into the floor to rise to starting position. Keep your ribs lifted. Lower back into a split squat. Do not let your knee push forward. Do two sets of 15, then switch sides.

SAFETY TIP: If your back knee hurts, straighten the back leg to decrease the stretch in the back thigh. If your front knee hurts, make sure your squatting is an up–down, not front–back movement.

Upper Body Shaper

a. Stand with your right leg in front. Lean on your thigh. Holding a weight in your left arm, hang your hand to the floor.

b. As you exhale, raise your elbow until your upper arm is horizontal. Turn your chest out.

c. Keep your upper arm still as you straighten your elbow. Hold, then lower the weight to the floor. Do two sets of 12, then switch sides.

SAFETY TIP: Support your lower back by leaning on your front leg.

Spine Strengthener

Lie face down, hands by your head. Extend your right arm out in front. As you exhale, raise your left thigh and right hand 3–6 inches off the floor. Hold until you feel the muscles in your back fatigue, lower. Do eight slowly. Switch sides.

SAFETY TIP: If you feel strain in your lower back, do not lift so high. Or rest on top of a chair and perform the exercise from a bent, rather than prone position, lifting only to horizontal, rather than arching the back.

Back Strengthener

Sit on a low chair with your feet flat. Lean forward, chin down. Place your hands with weights out in front. Exhale and lift your elbows back and up to the ceiling. Pull your shoulder blades closer to the spine. Lower. Do two sets of eight.

SAFETY TIP: Avoid rounding your back. Lean with a straight spine.

Shoulder Sculptor

Standing, hold a weight in each hand. Hold your right arm, palm down, in front of your thigh. Hold your left arm by your left thigh, palm in. Lift your ribs. Exhale and tighten your shoulders to raise your right arm to shoulder level in front and your left arm out to the side. Hold then slowly lower. Do two sets of 12, then switch sides.

SAFETY TIP: Avoid scrunching your shoulders to your ears.

Chest Builder

Lie on your back with a weight in each hand. Open your arms out to the side – hands turned sideways, palms facing your feet. Exhale, and bring your hands together above your chest. Lower slowly. Do two sets of 12.

SAFETY TIP: Try not to rotate your palms.

Lower Abdomen Flattener

a. Lie on your back and bring your right knee to your chest. Pull your bellybutton to your spine. Then push your left hand against your right knee to create resistance. Hold this position to stabilise your pelvis.

b. Without rocking your hips, slowly raise and lower your left foot. Tighten the abdominals in order to keep your balance. Do eight very slow leg raises, then switch sides.

SAFETY TIP: Remember to push your hand and knee against each other as you move the other leg.

Belly Firmer

Lie on your back and bend your knees. Hold a weight behind your head like a pillow. As you exhale, flatten your lower abdomen, then bring your ribcage towards your hips. Hold, then slowly pull your ribs away again. Repeat.

SAFETY TIP: Do not pull on your head to move forward. Rest your head back on the weight so your chin stays open.

WEEK FOUR
Eat More, Weigh Less Plan

DAY 22

Shopping list

FRUIT	VEGETABLES	
1 papaya	2 stalks broccoli	Corn salad
3 bananas	½lb spinach	Rocket
1 grapefruit	2 potatoes	Red peppers
3 apples	1 sweet potato	Yellow squash
4 oranges	Asparagus	Oatmeal
1 mango	Okra	Mushrooms
1 pint strawberries	Aubergine	Corn
1 cantaloup	Tomatoes	Brown rice
Grapes	Mangetout	Lentils
Lemon	Carrots	Artichokes
Lime	Watercress	

Menu

Eye-Opener	Fresh papaya
Energy Burst	Walk or dance for 5 minutes
Breakfast	Juicy fruit with cottage cheese
Snack	Fat-free popcorn
Lunch	Wholewheat sandwich with Cheddar, tomato and red peppers
Indulgence	2 scoops ice-cream
Snack	Carrots and cucumbers
Dinner	Broccoli, watercress & barley soup, fresh corn with lime, broccoli with lemon
Lite Snack	Grapefruit

Activity

Level 1:	20 mins fat-burning activity
Level 2:	35 mins fat-burning activity

Eating goal

Eat at least: 4 fresh pieces of fruit, 4 fresh vegetables, 1 serving of beans

DAY 23

Eye-Opener	Fresh-squeezed orange juice
Energy Burst	Walk or dance for 10 minutes
Breakfast	Granary toast and an egg
Snack	Banana
Lunch	Vegetable soup, green salad
Snack	Airpopped popcorn
Dinner	Spicy sesame rice noodles, oriental broccoli and mangetout, spiced rice, asparagus & carrots
Lite Snack	Apple

Activity

Level 1:	25 mins fat-burning activity
	metabolism-boosting exercises
Level 2:	30 mins fat-burning activity

Eating goal

Eat at least: 3 fresh pieces of fruit, 4 fresh vegetables, 1 wholegrain

DAY 24

Eye-Opener	Fresh cantaloupe
Energy Burst	Walk or dance for 10 minutes
Breakfast	Banana & almond oatmeal
Snack	Fat-free baked crisps
Lunch	Green salad, low-fat yoghurt
Snack	Apple
Dinner	Rocket & lentil soup, spiced rice and broccoli, yellow squash & red pepper
Lite Snack	Green grapes

Activity

Level 1:	20 mins fat-burning activity
Level 2:	40 mins fat-burning activity
	metabolism-boosting exercises

Eating goal

Eat at least: 4 fresh vegetables, 4 fresh pieces of fruit, 1 serving of beans and 1 wholegrain

DAY 25

Eye-Opener	Fresh-squeezed carrot juice
Energy Burst	Walk or dance for 5 minutes
Breakfast	Homemade muesli with skimmed milk
Snack	Apple
Lunch	Baked potato with beans & corn
Indulgence	Chocolate bar
Snack	Carrots
Dinner	Pasta with spring vegetables, green and yellow salad, roasted aubergine & courgette
Lite Snack	Strawberries

Activity

Level 1:	Have a rest day!
Level 2:	40 mins fat-burning activity

Eating goal

Eat at least: 4 fresh pieces of fruit, 3 fresh vegetables, 1 serving of beans

DAY 26

Eye-Opener	Fresh strawberries
Energy Burst	Walk or dance for 5 minutes
Breakfast	Tropical cottage cheese
Snack	Rice cakes
Lunch	Rye sandwich with cheese & salad
Snack	Carrots & sliced red peppers
Dinner	Sweet potatoes and turnips, steamed broccoli spinach with lemon, corn and barley soup
Lite Snack	Orange

Activity

Level 1:	30 mins fat-burning activity
Level 2:	metabolism-boosting exercises

Eating goal

Eat at least: 5 fresh pieces of fruit, 5 vegetables, 1 serving of beans

DAY 27

Eye-Opener	Fresh mango
Energy Burst	Walk or dance for 10 minutes
Breakfast	Apple cinnamon oatmeal
Snack	Fat-free crackers with cheese
Lunch	Steamed vegetables, brown rice
Snack	Banana
Dinner	Artichoke gratin, spinach & fresh pea salad, tomatoes with basil
Lite Snack	Carrot sticks

Activity

Level 1:	25 mins fat-burning activity
Level 2:	45 mins fat-burning activity
	metabolism-boosting exercises

Eating goal

Eat at least: 3 fresh vegetables, 4 fresh pieces of fruit, 1 serving of beans

DAY 28

Eye-Opener	Fresh-squeezed grapefruit juice
Energy Burst	Walk or dance for 10 minutes
Breakfast	Fruit with fromage frais
Snack	Strawberry, peach & pear smoothie
Lunch	Sweet potato, green salad
Snack	Baked crisps
Dinner	Okra & tomatoes, brown rice, spinach and split pea soup, steamed mangetout and carrots
Lite Snack	Green grapes

Activity

Level 1:	20 mins fat-burning activity
Level 2:	Have a rest day!

Eating goal

Eat at least: 3 fresh vegetables, 3 pieces of fresh fruit, 1 serving of beans

WEEK FOUR
Metabolism-Boosting Exercises

The following exercises will stretch and sculpt your major muscles. Do these 2–3 times a week according to the plan. Move slowly to control each movement. You'll see faster results if you use weights. Start with 2–3lb and work up to 5–10lb. Vary your weights as some muscles may be stronger than others.

Spine Relaxer
a. Stand with your feet shoulder width apart, toes forward, knees bent. Lean forward and rest your hands on your thighs. Press your chest out. Hold for 10 seconds.

b. As you exhale, drop your chin to your chest, tighten your abdominals and round your back. Feel your shoulder blades move apart. Hold for 10 seconds.
   SAFETY TIP: Support your lower back by leaning into your thighs.

Front Thigh Stretch

Place your right foot on a bench or chair and bend your front knee. Press your left hip forwards. Hold for 15–20 seconds, then switch legs.

SAFETY TIP: If you feel pain in your knee, straighten your back leg.

Back Thigh Stretch

Place your right leg on a bench or chair. Rest your hands on your thigh. Lean slightly forward as you push your hips out behind. Hold for 15–30 seconds, then lift your toe. Hold 15 seconds, then switch sides.

SAFETY TIP: If your thigh feels overstretched, bend the knee.

Arm & Shoulder Stretch

Stand or sit and raise your right arm as you hold onto the elbow with your left hand. Bend the right elbow and gently pull on your arm. Lower the right arm in front of your chest and pull the right elbow towards the left shoulder. Hold 10 seconds, then switch sides.

SAFETY TIP: Do not bounce.

Buttocks Shaper

a. Stand with your feet parallel, shoulder width apart. Lean at a diagonal with a straight back and lower your hips. Holding weights, bring your hands to your shoulders.

b. As you exhale, squeeze your buttocks and straighten to standing. As you do so kick your right thigh out to the side and slowly straighten your elbows. Hold, then lower. Do two sets of 15. Then switch sides.

SAFETY TIP: If you feel stress in your knees, ensure that your body weight is in your heels, not toes when you squat. Look down at your feet and make sure you can always see your toes.

Inner Thigh Lift

Lie on your left side and prop yourself up on your elbow. Bend your right knee, foot flat and extend your left leg out. Turn your left foot out to the side. Hold a weight on your inner thigh. As you exhale, squeeze your inner thigh and raise your leg towards the ceiling. Then slowly lower. Do two sets of 15, then switch sides.

SAFETY TIP: Do not let your ribs sag to the ground; hold your torso upright.

Upper Body Strengthener

a. Stand tall with your knees soft. Hold a weight in your right hand on your shoulder, palm facing forward.

b. As you exhale, extend your arm to the upper right corner of the ceiling so your arm makes a diagonal as you pull your elbow into your ribs. Do 12 slowly, then switch sides.

SAFETY TIP: Focus on pulling your shoulder blades towards your spine.

Upper Arm Firmer

a. Sit or stand with your ribs lifted, spine tall. Holding a weight in both hands, raise your arms over your head then bend your elbows and drop your hands behind your shoulders.

b. As you exhale, straighten your arms and push the weight up to the ceiling. Keep the upper arm stable as you move the lower arm. Then slowly bend. Do two sets of 12.

SAFETY TIP: Press your elbows close to your head.

Waist Lift

Lie on your left side with your left arm along the front of your body. Hold your right hand behind your head. As you exhale, lift sideways so that you bring your ribcage closer to your hips. This is a very subtle movement. Do eight slowly, then switch sides.

SAFETY TIP: Avoid pulling on your neck; instead compress the waist to your side to bend.

Lower Abdominal Curl

Lie on your back and bend your knees into your chest. Hold your hands by your sides. Hold a weight between your knees. As you exhale, first flatten your lower abdomen, then bring your hips and ribs together. Hold, then slowly lower your tailbone. Repeat. Try not to swing your legs or lift your back off the ground.

SAFETY TIP: Do not open and close your thighs; keep them close to your chest.

Breast Lifter

a. Lie on your stomach and place your hands underneath your shoulders, fingers forward. Curl your toes under and prop your body up so that your elbows, knees and back are straight.

b. As you inhale, bend your elbows and lower your chest. Exhale and push back up. Rather than doing this on your knees, try to do 1–3 perfect push-ups. Then add more as you grow stronger.

   SAFETY TIP: Pull your bellybutton in to support your back.

DON'T FAST, FEAST

Fasting is bad for you. Fasting is a prime example of how eating *less* can eventually cause you to weigh *more* – among other problems. Although many trendy diet plans suggest that you can 'detoxify' yourself by depriving yourself of food for a few days, in reality you could cause your body great damage.

The body has an incredible ability to adapt to stressful situations. Fasting is a type of stress. Since you are literally starving yourself, your body has to cope to preserve much-needed energy. This can have long-term consequences for your health and your weight. Your normal balancing mechanisms are thrown off track. Your body is in a state of emergency because it does not have the raw materials it needs to work properly. So it compensates in whatever way it can.

Your body needs energy every minute to function. Even after just five or six hours of not eating (whether from fasting or skipping a meal), the body feels as if it is being starved. In response it draws upon its stored energy sources: carbohydrates, fat and protein. Although you generally have an endless supply of fat for energy, the blood, your muscles and your brain rely on stored carbohydrates, or glycogen. These stores are depleted within a day. As a fast continues, your body's needs for carbohydrates does not diminish, but their availability does. So your body goes into panic mode and starts taking protein from your muscle fibres and converting it into the carbohydrates that your brain and body desperately need. This makes you physically weaker.

When your energy demands are still not met by refuelling (eating), your liver then breaks down fat into a chemical form of energy that the brain can use. This helps preserve some of the body's protein stores because otherwise you can die from losing too much protein.

Not Eating Slows Your Metabolism

Just as a computer goes into 'sleep' mode when it's turned on but you haven't used it for a while, so your body utilises a similar energy-preservation mechanism. The metabolism slows down, the body temperature cools, and the muscles do less work. The body improves its ability to hold on to its fat reserves. Not only is your body thrown completely out of rhythm, but the physical symptoms you suffer as this happens include headaches, fatigue and weakness.

Meanwhile even more serious forms of nutritional depletion are occurring. Calcium is lost from the bones – a very dangerous situation for men and women prone to osteoporosis. Your body tries to conserve water, and in doing so loses potassium. The loss of too much potassium impairs nerve transmission from the brain to the muscles. Cramping and muscle weakness is a common symptom. This can even cause the heart to stop.

Since you are not ingesting the daily requirements of nutrients that you get from foods including Vitamin C, the B vitamins and over two dozen minerals, your immune system, energy levels and the state of your hair, skin and nails may be affected.

In addition, fasting causes increases in blood cholesterol and thyroid hormone, which helps you regulate the use and storage of fat. The protein stores and muscle mass you lose during the fast mean that when you start eating normally again, you will gain weight very easily. Since your metabolism has slowed down, *eating less* can now make you *gain* weight.

If you do not absorb enough calories for energy, your body will simply not function properly at any level, from cell repair and renewal, to thinking clearly or moving. The longer you fast, the harder it becomes to eat. You lose your appetite because your body literally tenses up. Even if you force yourself to eat, your body is not in a receptive state to digest the food properly. Not only are you setting yourself up for illness when you fast or go on very low-calorie diets, you are also creating a scenario where, instead of losing weight, your body is learning how to hold on to it.

Dieting Can Trigger a Fasting Response

What most people don't realise is that diets where you selectively rearrange the types of food you eat can have the same effect. A low-carbohydrate diet will also result in the same lack of fuel to the brain. The same wasting process that occurs during fasting will take effect in order to compensate. A high-protein diet aims to prevent the wasting loss of muscle protein while the body is in a fasting state of low or no carbohydrates. But studies have shown that this approach is not effective. There is still not enough fuel for the brain.

Any low-calorie or carbohydrate-sparing diet will have disastrous effects on the body. Your brain alone requires up to 600 calories a day. When you do not meet your vitamin, mineral and energy needs, your body suffers. When you eat a diet high in junk and low in nutrients, your body is also deprived and you will feel and look the worse for it. That's why it's crucial to eat more, and to eat better.

Many people don't eat breakfast. This is a big mistake. After having slept and not eaten for 7–10 hours, then gone another three or four waking hours without any food, your body is put into a precarious fasting state. The initial stages of starvation have begun. Although you might eat well later in the day, months – or even years – of subjecting your body to this daily stress takes its toll. Research has shown that both children and adults benefit in the short and long term from regularly eating breakfast. Even if you prefer not to eat a big meal when you wake up, at least eat some fruit.

The 3-Day ANTI-FAST Feast

If you would like a healthy jumpstart to help you focus on eating well, instead of fasting, try feasting. Rather than try to clear out your system and deny it what it needs, try replenishing your body with all the nutrients it lacks.

Once you've tried the 28-day *Eat More, Weigh Less*

plan, you may want to periodically rejuvenate yourself by feasting or stuffing yourself with as many life-giving nutrients as possible. The following food and activity plan lasts three days. Even if your schedule does not permit you to eat completely healthily all the time, if you can squeeze high-nutrient eating and healthy amounts of exercise into three days of your week you can greatly improve the quality of your life and looks. Rather than fasting, and putting your body into a precarious, vulnerable physical and mental state, focus on feeding your body what it needs.

The plan is similar in structure to the 28-day *Eat More, Weigh Less* plan. It also includes daily activities, so if these three days are the only days you manage to exercise each week, you'll still be able to maintain a dedicated fitness programme and, of course, reap the rewards by looking and feeling better, and maintaining, or even losing, weight and body fat.

You can choose any of the metabolism-boosting exercises given during the 28-day plan. It's a good idea to periodically vary the types of activities you do.

THE 3-DAY ANTI-FAST FEAST

DAY 1

Shopping list

FRUIT	VEGETABLES	
3 bananas	2 stalks broccoli	Split peas
1 grapefruit	½lb spinach	Lentils
3 apples	2 potatoes	Red beans
4 oranges	1 sweet potato	Corn salad
1 mango	Asparagus	Rocket
1 pint strawberries	Mangetout	Watercress
Melon	Okra	Carrots
Grapes	Tomatoes	Oatmeal
Peach	Red & yellow peppers	Brown rice
Nectarine	Almonds	
Blueberries	Rice cakes	
Papaya	Couscous	

Menu

Eye-Opener	Fresh cantaloupe
Energy Burst	Walk or dance for 15 minutes
Breakfast	Juice fruit with cottage cheese
Snack	Strawberry & banana smoothie
Lunch	Green salad, vegetable soup
Snack	Carrots
Dinner	Brown rice with lentils; spinach, tomato & red pepper salad; steamed broccoli & mangetout
Lite Snack	Nectarine

Activity

Level 1:	20 mins fat-burning activity metabolism-boosting exercises
Level 2:	30 mins fat-burning activity metabolism-boosting exercises

Eating goal

Eat at least: 5 vegetables, 4 fresh pieces of fruit, 1 bean, 1 grain

DAY 2

Menu

Eye-Opener	Fresh mango
Energy Burst	Walk or dance for 15 minutes
Breakfast	Banana & almond oatmeal
Snack	Grapes, strawberries & blueberries
Lunch	Green salad, low-fat yoghurt
Snack	Melon
Dinner	Sweet potato, almost raw vegetable salad, spinach & roasted red peppers, carrot & split pea soup
Lite Snack	Apple

Activity

Level 1:   15 mins fat-burning activity
Level 2:   40 mins fat-burning activity

Eating goal

Eat at least: 5 vegetables, 4 fresh pieces of fruit, 1 bean, 1 grain

DAY 3

Eye-Opener	Fresh papaya
Energy Burst	Walk or dance for 15 minutes
Breakfast	Low-fat yoghurt with banana, oat & barley flakes
Snack	Fresh-squeezed orange & grapefruit juice
Lunch	Baked potato with corn salad
Snack	Carrots & sliced red peppers
Dinner	3-bean salad, red pepper couscous, steamed asparagus & broccoli
Lite Snack	Strawberries and blueberries

Activity

Level 1: 20 mins fat-burning activity
metabolism-boosting exercises

Level 2: 30 mins fat-burning activity
metabolism-boosting exercises

Eating goal

Eat at least: 5 vegetables, 4 fresh pieces of fruit, 1 bean, 1 grain

PART THREE

USING BEANS

Beans are ingenious parcels of energy and nutrients. But they have an undeserved bad reputation. Although most people are quite content to eat red kidney beans, and the odd lentil dal in an Indian restaurant, they shy away from using beans as a regular staple in their diet. Many fear flatulence, although this is only caused when beans are cooked incorrectly. Many people think they are difficult to prepare. In fact, like grains, they are easy to cook – all you do is boil them.

You can buy some beans fresh in the pod. These include broad beans, peas, soybeans and black-eyed peas. These are ideal because they take about 10 minutes to steam, like other fresh vegetables. But they're not always available. Most beans come in a dried form in which they retain their high nutrient value and can be stored for long periods. You can use them instead of meat for most recipes and they are highly filling and delicious. They come in a multitude of different flavours, textures, shapes, colours and sizes. Canned beans are a convenient and nutritious option as well, though some of the nutrients may leak out into the water they are stored in.

Because dried beans are such a dense, compact,

energy source some can take a long time to cook. Some small beans, such as lentils and mung beans, are amazingly quick to cook – about 25 minutes. Others, such as black beans, red beans or butter beans, take longer.

There are several ways to cook beans. You can *greatly* reduce the cooking time if you soak the beans before you cook them. This does not require as much effort as it sounds. All you do is put a serving of dried beans in a bowl of hot water, cover and leave them to soak in ten times the quantity of water for 4–8 hours, depending upon the bean. It's very easy to put a new batch in a bowl when you're clearing up dinner the night before, or when you're eating breakfast before you go off to work. Change the soaking water periodically. This removes the toxins which are responsible for excess gas in your intestines. Cooking them thoroughly will also alleviate the problem. After the beans are soaked, rinse them thoroughly before cooking.

You can use a quick-soak method by boiling the beans in water for 10–15 minutes, then letting them soak in that water for three hours before you cook. When you cook beans in a normal pot you let them simmer for the allotted time, or until tender. Older beans may take longer to cook.

The easiest way to cook beans is with a pressure cooker. This is a large pot with a lid that seals on tight. The pressure builds up inside, helping them to cook faster. You can cut the cooking time in half for most beans by using this method, and you don't have to pre-soak them.

No matter which way you cook your beans, never use salt, either in the soaking or cooking water. This will toughen the skin of the beans, making them very difficult to cook. Cover the beans with at least two inches of fresh water. Boil the water, then reduce the heat and simmer them until they are tender. Some of the faster cooking beans such as lentils, mung beans and aduki beans can be cooked in the same pot as your grains. Fresh beans should be stored in the refrigerator, dried beans in an airtight container in a cool cupboard. Once they're cooked, keep them in the refrigerator for 3–5 days. For convenience sake, it's always a good idea to make a larger serving of grains or beans and store them in the refrigerator so you have ready-cooked portions for a couple of days.

Beans are the ideal diet food: they are very filling and give substance to your meal, yet they are high in fibre, very low in fat and extremely nutritious.

Chart 8:
Cooking Beans

Dried beans	Cooking time after soaking	In pressure cooker (minutes)
Aduki	30–60 minutes	12
Black beans	1½ hours	20
Blackeyed peas	45 minutes	12
Butterbeans	1½ hours	17
Lima beans	1½ hours	20
Cannellini	1 hour	25
Chick peas	1½–2 hours	20
Flageolet	1 hour	15
Haricot	1–1½ hours	20
Lentils	25 minutes	12
Mung beans	30 minutes	12
Red kidney beans	1–1½ hours	20
Borlotti beans	1 hour	17
Soybeans	3–4 hours	30
Fava (broad)	4 hours	45
Split peas	1 hour	20

* 2 cups of dried beans will make about 6 cups of cooked beans

USING GRAINS

Grains are one of the earth's most abundant foods. They are complex carbohydrates low in calories and fat, rich in B vitamins, fibre, protein, minerals and a host of phytochemicals. All cultures throughout the ages have relied on local grains as their main food source. In the twentieth-century West, we have tended to use grains that have been refined, or highly processed so that much of their nutritious value is removed. Instead of eating wholewheat grain in its natural form, we have processed wheat grains into flour, removing the hull and germ of the grain and taking out much of the nutrients and fibre along the way. Bread, breakfast cereal and pasta, staples for most people, contain refined wheat. Bread and pasta are good food choices, but it's healthier to return to eating grains in their natural unrefined state.

Grains come in a variety of textures and tastes, but they are all very chewy and filling. They can be served hot or cold, sweet or savoury. Barley grains are light and neutral tasting, but have a juicy texture which adds a nice element to soups. Rye grains have a heavier and stronger flavour, perfect for warm savoury dishes. Even rice comes in many different varieties – long-grain red rice is heavy and chewy with a nutty taste; plain brown rice is light and has a neutral taste. You may be surprised to know that you can also buy wholewheat kernels. These have an almost identical texture to brown rice, but are slightly more succulent.

You can – and should – eat whole grains regularly. The food pyramid guidelines recommending six to eleven servings a day of grain foods should include *at least* three servings of whole grains. So you shouldn't focus just on eating pasta and bread, but should also eat brown rice, barley, oats and other grains.

Grains which have been crushed into flakes can be added to muesli, or cooked into a hot cereal. These come not only in oat flakes or porridge, but in rye, barley and other flakes as well. Grains in their whole, kernel form are often referred to as 'groats'. So oat groats or wheat groats are simply the original form of a grain that resembles a kernel of rice and can be boiled in the same way. Grains are also refined into flour, then used in baked or processed foods. Try to use wholegrain flour when possible so that more of the nutrients are retained.

Grains go with just about anything, including all vegetables beans, meat, poultry and fish. You can use most grains in the same way as you do rice. Grains are easy to prepare. Anyone can cook them: all you do is boil them in water. As long as you plan your meal preparation efficiently, they can be just as fast and easy to use as pasta. If you immediately put the grains on the stove to cook while you're preparing the rest of the food, they'll be ready by the time you sit down to eat. For convenience, make an extra-large batch that you can keep in the refrigerator.

Chart 9:
Cooking Grains

Grain	Water	Cooking time (minutes)
Barley	3–4 cups	30
Buckwheat	2 cups	20
Cornmeal	4 cups	25
Millet	3–4 cups	45
Oats	2 cups	20
Rice	2 cups	45–50
Wild rice	3 cups	60
Rye (whole)	4 cups	60
Rye (flakes)	2 cups	20
Wheat (cracked)	2 cups	25
Wheat (bulgur)	2 cups	15
Wheat (flakes)	2 cups	20–25
Wheat (couscous)	2 cups	See note*
Quinoa	2 cups	15–20

* Add couscous to 1 cup boiling water, remove from heat, cover and let sit for 5 minutes.

Cooking time will vary according to the size and density of the grain. Tiny, light grains such as barley and quinoa cook very fast (5–10 minutes), while heavier, bigger grains like brown rice and wheat kernels take longer (10–30 minutes). In general you use 2–3 parts salted water to 1 part of the grain. Bring the water and grain to the boil, then lower the heat and simmer until the texture is soft. If you soak a grain, like rice, covered, for 30 minutes before cooking, you will greatly reduce the cooking time. You can also cook them in the oven, but this takes longer.

There are many varieties of grains (and seeds which are similar to grains), so you need never get bored. Different grains and forms of grains include: amarynth, barley, buckwheat, millet, oats, quinoa, rye, wheat, couscous, kasha, polenta and bulgur wheat.

USING VEGETABLES

Most people stick to familiar vegetables such as lettuce, cucumbers, potatoes and tomatoes. But vegetables are one of the most important nutrient sources, so it is vital to incorporate a large variety of them in your diet. The *Eat More, Weigh Less* plan is filled with vegetables of all colours, shapes and sizes. Some of the menu items on the 28-day plan are included in this recipe section. Others are simply different combinations of steamed vegetables, so they require no recipe. Since some nutrients can be lost from heat and water exposure, it is important to try to minimise the cooking time by keeping the temperature hot and the water low. If you do not find a recipe for a vegetable dish listed on the plan, cook it as follows:

1. Wash the vegetables to remove dirt and some pesticides. If it is a root vegetable, such as a turnip, carrot or potato, you may wish to use a vegetable brush to scrub the surface.

2. Cut the vegetables into smaller pieces if necessary. Some items like carrots, broccoli, cauliflower, okra and beets will cook faster if you cut them, since they

are very dense. Others such as mangetout, asparagus and spinach do not need to be cut.

3. Using an inch or so of water in a pan, bring it to a rapid boil before introducing the vegetables.

4. Place veggies in bamboo or metal steamer if possible. If not, place them in the water for as short a time as possible. Covering the pot can increase the temperature to reduce cooking time, but some cruciferous vegetables such as broccoli, Brussels sprouts and cabbage will lose flavour and colour if covered. You can steam corn while still in its husk: this will make it dramatically sweeter.

5. Most vegetables will take 5–10 minutes maximum to cook, depending upon whether you like them crispy or tender. As long as you cut the denser vegetables into smaller pieces, or put them in first for a few minutes, you can put all your veggies together in the same pot to save time and washing-up.

6. Eat immediately. If you are cooking an elaborate meal, steam the veggies last so they can be served hot.

You can also stir-fry, microwave or bake vegetables. If you stir-fry, do not slather the wok or frying pan in oil. Even though olive oil is nutritious, it is very high in calories. Microwaving can retain more of the nutrients; experiment to find the minimum cooking times needed. Baking takes longer and so may deplete some of the more heat-sensitive vitamins.

MAKING SALADS

To many people, a salad is a highly fattening concoction of mayonnaise and oil with a few canned vegetables or beans thrown in. These salads, served in many restaurant 'salad bars', are not only very high in calories: they are often not very nutritious.

If you are used to this kind of salad, redefine what you perceive a salad to be. It should be a low-fat mixture of a variety of raw and/or slightly steamed vegetables. A light dressing should enhance but not overtake the flavour of the individual ingredients.

Raw vegetables in salads are a great source of nutrients because none are lost through the cooking process. They are virtually fat-free and very low in calories. So get adventurous with your salads and make them more colourful than the usual iceberg lettuce and tomato version. The *Eat More, Weigh Less* plan has several different salads, but you can also invent your own, adding as many *different* ingredients as you can.

Raw vegetables you can use include:

all types of lettuce	go for the dark green leafy variety when possible
spinach	carrots
cucumbers	tomatoes

beets	peas
mangetout	mushrooms
broccoli	cauliflower
avocado	red, green and yellow peppers
turnips	watercress
bean sprouts	onions
baby corns	red, white and green cabbage

If you prefer your veggies cooked, you can steam many vegetables so that they are tender. Let them cool, then add them to your salad. Lightly steamed vegetables you can add include:

asparagus	broccoli
sweet peppers	mangetout
carrots	sugar snap peas
fresh corn	beets

You can also use beans and some grains such as couscous to add a little substance to your salad. You may find that canned artichoke hearts, palm hearts, capers, and even jalapeno peppers can spice up your salad.

RECIPES

The following pages give the recipes for menu items included in your 28-day *Eat More, Weigh Less* plan and the 3-day *Anti-Fast* Feast. These recipes were designed with an emphasis on a wide variety of nutrient-rich, fresh foods. The recipes are vegetarian-based, but you can add meat, fish and poultry according to the serving options given.

Each recipe is low in fat, but rather than the usual diet fare, contains revitalising ingredients. A nutritional breakdown is given showing the percentage and amount of fat, carbohydrates, protein and calories in each dish, as well as a notation of the particular nutrients present in each recipe.

You may modify the recipes according to your own particular needs, likes and dislikes. Since some of the fruit and vegetables suggested are seasonal or may not be available to you, substitute similar items when necessary. For example, if strawberries are out of season, substitute another fruit high in vitamin C such as oranges or melon. The emphasis in this food plan is variety, so make sure to experiment with different types of fruit, vegetables, beans and grains.

Since it is likely that you have not included many

grains and beans in your diet in the past, pay particular attention to experimenting with different types. You may need to go to a health food store for the obscure grains, but most should be available at your local supermarket. Most grains and beans are interchangeable. The food plan tends to stick with the most common such as brown rice, lentils, barley and kidney beans. Once you are familiar with using these, substitute others. Don't worry if you are unsure about how to cook beans and grains; the next few pages will give you tips on how to prepare them.

Note: All recipes will use the following conversions:
1 cup = 8oz = 240 ml
1oz = 30g

Almost Raw Vegetable Salad

Serves 3

4 cups water
4 cups vegetables including broccoli, red pepper, carrots, mushrooms, cauliflower, green beans
¼ cup low-fat Italian dressing

Boil water. Add vegetables for just 5 minutes so they stay crunchy. Drain immediately. Toss vegetables with dressing, and chill in the refrigerator for one hour.

Nutritional breakdown per serving

359 kcal – 1503 KJ
Protein 24g
Fat 9g
Carbohydrates 46g

Especially high in most vitamins and minerals except vitamin B12 and vitamin D

Apple Cinnamon Oatmeal

Serves 2

1 apple sliced
½ teaspoon cinnamon
½ teaspoon allspice
½ teaspoon sugar
½ cup oats
½ cup skimmed milk or ½ cup water

Mix the oats with the water or milk and boil. Add spices, sugar and sliced apple. Simmer for 5 minutes, stirring occasionally.

Nutritional breakdown per serving

279 kcal – 1181 KJ
Protein 9g
Fat 6g
Carbohydrates 52g

Especially high in vitamin B1 and calcium

Apple-Oatmeal Pancakes

Serves 3

1 cup rolled oats, cooked
½ cup wholewheat flour
1 teaspoon baking soda
1 cup buttermilk
2 egg whites
1 tablespoon apple juice

Combine all dry ingredients. In a separate small bowl, mix the buttermilk, egg whites and apple juice. Stir this mixture into the dry ingredients. Drop spoonfuls of the batter on to a hot non-stick griddle. Cook for one minute on each side, until golden.

Nutritional breakdown per serving

205 kcal – 1872 KJ
Protein 11g
Fat 2g
Carbohydrates 38g

Especially high in vitamins B1, B2 and folate

Serves 6

1¼lb (625g) Jerusalem artichokes
½ large chopped onion
2 crushed garlic cloves
1 tablespoon olive oil
4 courgettes
3 large tomatoes (peeled and chopped)
½ teaspoon fennel seeds
2oz (60g) grated Cheddar cheese

Peel the artichokes and cut into bite-sized pieces. Simmer in water until nearly tender, then drain and set aside. Sauté the onion in the oil with the crushed garlic until soft. Slice the courgettes and add to the pan. Sauté for 5 minutes before adding the tomatoes and the fennel seeds. Scatter the surface with the grated cheese and put into the pre-heated oven at 375°F (190°C, Gas mark 5) for 30 minutes, turning the temperature up to 400°F (200°C, Gas mark 6) for the last 5 minutes to brown top.

Nutritional breakdown per serving

109 kcal – 490 KJ
Protein 6g
Fat 4g
Carbohydrates 15g

Especially high in most nutrients, including B1, B6, folate, vitamins A, C and E

Baked Apple Fluff

Serves 5

5 green cooking apples
pared rind of 1 lemon
4–5 egg whites (size 3)
4oz (120g) caster sugar

Peel, core and quarter the apples and place them in a saucepan with about 4 tablespoons water and the lemon rind. Cover and cook gently until they are tender and fluffy, then leave them to cool and remove the lemon rind. Whisk until light. Beat the egg whites until they are quite stiff, then add the sugar gradually until it is a firm froth. Fold the apples into the meringue. Heap the mixture in a glass dish and serve with cream.

Nutritional breakdown per serving

149 kcal – 639 KJ
Protein 3g
Fat trace
Carbohydrates 36g

Especially high in vitamin C

Serves 2

1 banana, sliced
½ cup oats
½ teaspoon cinnamon
½ teaspoon brown sugar
1–1¼ cups water

Mix the oats with the water and boil. Add cinnamon, sugar and sliced banana. Simmer for 5 minutes, stirring occasionally.

Nutritional breakdown per serving

286 kcal – 1213 KJ
Protein 8g
Fat 6g
Carbohydrates 55g

Especially high in vitamin B1

Basic Brown Rice

Serves 3

1 cup brown rice
2½ cups water
¾ teaspoon salt

Bring rice and water to a rolling boil. Add ¾ teaspoon salt, if desired. Cover and simmer: 15–20 minutes for Basmati or Texmatic rice; 45 minutes for long-grain rice. Do not lift the lid until the cooking time is up. Fluff with fork.

Nutritional breakdown per serving

286 kcal – 1214 KJ
Protein 5g
Fat 2g
Carbohydrates 65g

Especially high in vitamin B1, foliate and magnesium

Serves 4

1 cup cooked kidney beans
1 cup cooked blackeyed peas
1 cup cooked barley
2 corn on the cobs
1½ teaspoons chopped garlic
6 tomatoes
1 cup water
1 teaspoon chilli powder
1 teaspoon dried basil
1 teaspoon dried oregano
½ teaspoon pepper
1 teaspoon cumin
1 cup chopped carrots
1 cup chopped celery
1 medium onion

Combine the ingredients. Bring to a boil then reduce heat and simmer, covered, for 10 minutes. Stir in vegetables and cook for 10 minutes.

For extra calcium and a thicker texture, you can add skimmed milk in place of some water.

Nutritional breakdown per serving

229 kcal – 972 KJ
Protein 15g
Fat 2g
Carbohydrates 42g

Especially high in most vitamins and minerals except vitamins B12 and D

Blackeyed Beans and Corn

Serves 6

1½ cups blackeyed beans
5 tomatoes
1 chopped onion
1 clove crushed garlic
3 cups water
¼ cup chopped basil
¼ cup parsley
2 ears of corn on the cob

Soak beans in water overnight. Drain, then place in a pan with enough water to cover. Boil for 30 minutes then drain. Boil or steam the corn then cut the kernel off each cob. Combine beans, crushed tomatoes, onion, garlic and water in a large saucepan. Boil, reduce heat, cover and simmer for an hour until beans are tender. Add the parsley, basil and corn, then simmer for 10 more minutes.

Nutritional breakdown per serving

227 kcal – 966 KJ
Protein 16g
Fat 2g
Carbohydrates 40g

Especially high in most vitamins and minerals except vitamins B12 and D

Serves 2

4 stalks broccoli
2 cups water
1 teaspoon salt
1 lemon

Either put fresh broccoli through a juicer to separate the juice and pulp, or chop and blend with a small amount of water to liquefy. If you have juiced the broccoli, boil the water and pulp together for 10 minutes. Add the raw broccoli juice and cook for the last 3 minutes, then add lemon juice and salt to taste. If you have the blended liquid, boil, then simmer for 10 minutes.

For extra calcium and a thicker texture, you can add skimmed milk in place of some water.

Nutritional breakdown per serving

81 kcal – 336 KJ
Protein 11g
Fat 2g
Carbohydrates 5g

Especially high in folate, iron, vitamins A, C and E

Serves 4

2 stalks broccoli, chopped
1 cup barley
2 small potatoes, cubed
2 tomatoes
2 cups water
1 teaspoon pepper
1 cup chopped carrots
1 medium onion

Combine half of the broccoli, and all of the potatoes, carrots, onion, tomatoes, barley, pepper and water. Bring to the boil. Reduce heat and simmer, covered, for 30 minutes. Stir in remainder of the broccoli and cook for 10 minutes. Salt to taste.

For extra calcium and a thicker texture, you can add skimmed milk in place of some water.

Nutritional breakdown per serving

166 kcal – 699 KJ
Protein 8g
Fat 2g
Carbohydrates 31g

Especially high in all B vitamins; also vitamins A, C and E

Serves 2

½ tablespoon olive oil
4oz (100g) chopped onion
12oz (350g) chopped broccoli
1½ tablespoons chopped fresh basil
1 teaspoon tamari
salt and pepper
2 large tomatoes (scoop out centre and save)
12 fresh basil leaves
4 cherry tomatoes

Heat oil and fry onion until soft. Add broccoli and cook covered for 10 minutes or until tender. Add the basil and tamari and combine. Season, then blend in a blender. Use an ice-cream scoop to form four broccoli balls. Divide the remaining broccoli mixture between the four tomato shells, and press into each base. Arrange three basil leaves around the edge to form petals. Place the broccoli ball on top, then garnish with a cherry tomato.

Nutritional breakdown per serving

138 kcal – 577 KJ
Protein 10g
Fat 6g
Carbohydrates 12g

Especially high in vitamins B, A, C, iron and folate

Serves 8

1 cup chopped broccoli
1 cup chopped watercress
1 cup barley
1½ teaspoons chopped garlic
4 tomatoes
3 cups water
1 teaspoon dried basil
1 teaspoon dried oregano
1 cup chopped carrots
1 cup chopped celery
½ teaspoon pepper
salt to taste

Combine watercress, barley, water, garlic, tomatoes, carrots, celery and herbs in a pot of water. Bring to the boil. Reduce heat and simmer, covered, for 10 minutes. Stir in broccoli and cook for 10 minutes.

For extra calcium and a thicker texture, you can add skimmed milk in place of some water.

Nutritional breakdown per serving

144 kcal – 613 KJ
Protein 5g
Fat 1g
Carbohydrates 30g

Especially high in vitamins A, C, B1 and folate

Serves 4

1 can or 1 cup dried butterbeans
4–6 small new potatoes, sliced
1 teaspoon butter
salt and pepper to taste

Boil beans and potatoes separately. Combine and add butter, salt and pepper to taste.

Nutritional breakdown per serving

109 kcal – 460 KJ
Protein 7g
Fat 2g
Carbohydrates 18g

Especially high in iron and all the B vitamins

Cappellini with Fresh Tomato & Basil

Serves 6

2lb fresh plum tomatoes, seeded and chopped
½ cup fresh basil leaves, chopped
4 tablespoons sherry vinegar
4 tablespoons bottled capers
freshly ground pepper
½lb cappellini or angel hair pasta
½ tablespoon olive oil
fresh basil leaves for garnish

Combine tomato and basil in a bowl; marinate at room temperature for 1–2 hours or overnight. Combine vinegar, capers and pepper with tomatoes.

In a large pot, bring water to a rapid boil. Add pasta and cook *al dente*. Drain well. Transfer pasta to a platter and toss with oil. Stir in tomato mixture and allow to stand for 5 minutes before serving. Garnish with basil leaves.

Nutritional breakdown per serving

544 kcal – 2313 KJ
Protein 18g
Fat 8g
Carbohydrates 106g

Especially high in folate, vitamins B1, B6, A, C and E

Carrot & Pea Soup

Serves 4

6oz (180g) onion, finely chopped
1 crushed garlic clove
1 vegetable stock cube
1lb (480g) diced carrots
1 tablespoon fresh chopped mint
2 teaspoons chopped fresh thyme
1oz (30g) ground almonds
2 pts boiling water
salt and pepper
1lb (480g) peas

Steam the onion until soft. Add the garlic, cook for a minute, then mix in the stock cube. Stir in the carrots and herbs, then cover and cook a further 5 minutes. Add the almonds, remove the pan from the heat and slowly stir in the water. Return the pan to the heat, season and bring to the boil. Add the peas, cover, bring back to the boil, and simmer for 3 minutes.

For extra calcium and a thicker texture, you can add skimmed milk in place of some water.

Nutritional breakdown per serving

213 kcal – 886 KJ
Protein 12g
Fat 7g
Carbohydrates 28g

Especially high in iron, folate, vitamins A, C, E, B1 and B6 and vitamin D

Chana Dal

Serves 4

8oz (240g) yellow split peas
5 garlic cloves
1 teaspoon turmeric
1-inch (2½cm) stick cinnamon
3 cloves
salt
citrus juice
teaspoon cumin seeds

Soak split peas in hot water for 30 minutes (removing any stones). Rinse several times. Peel and slice the garlic.

Boil peas in 2 pints of water. Remove scum, reduce heat, add half the garlic along with the turmeric, cinnamon and cloves. Simmer gently, partially covered, for about 45 minutes or until tender. Mash dal, adding more water until it is the desired consistency. Season with salt and citrus juice. Fry remaining garlic until golden. Add cumin, stir well and pour over dal.

Nutritional breakdown per serving

200 kcal – 853 KJ
Protein 14g
Fat 2g
Carbohydrates 35g

Especially high in vitamin B1 and iron

Chunky Vegetable Soup

Serves 4

2 potatoes
4 cups water
1 vegetable stock cube
1 stalk broccoli
2 carrots
4 medium aubergines
1 red pepper, cubed

Stir the water and stock cube together and boil. Add potatoes, carrots and aubergines and simmer for 10 minutes. Add broccoli and red pepper and cook for an additional 10 minutes.

For extra calcium and a thicker texture, you can add skimmed milk in place of some water.

You can add lean ham or beef to this soup.

Nutritional breakdown per serving

97 kcal – 411 KJ
Protein 4g
Fat 1g
Carbohydrates 18g

Especially high in vitamins A and C

Corn & Barley Soup

Serves 6

1 cup barley
2 corn on the cobs
2 potatoes, cubed
1½ teaspoons chopped garlic
4 tomatoes
3 cups water
1 teaspoon dried basil
½ teaspoon pepper
1 teaspoon cumin
1 cup chopped carrots

Steam corn on the cobs separately. When cooked, cut off kernels with a knife. Combine barley, water, potatoes, tomatoes, carrots, garlic and seasonings. Bring to a boil. Reduce heat and simmer, covered, for 20 minutes. Stir in corn and cook for 10 minutes.

For extra calcium and a thicker texture, you can add skimmed milk in place of some water.

You can add shredded chicken breast to this dish.

Nutritional breakdown per serving

290 kcal – 1233 KJ
Protein 8g
Fat 3g
Carbohydrates 63g

Especially high in vitamins B1, B6, folate, A and C

Serves 4

6 cups red and green cabbage
2 lemons
½ cup low-fat Italian dressing

Chop cabbage into thin shreds. Mix with the lemon juice and dressing.

Nutritional breakdown per serving

108 kcal – 455 KJ
Protein 5g
Fat 2g
Carbohydrates 19g

Especially high in vitamins B1, B6, folate and C

Four-bean Salad

Serves 4

1 cup fresh green beans
1 can chickpeas
1 can kidney beans
1 cup mangetout
3 tablespoons red wine vinegar
3 tomatoes
1 sliced carrot

Combine beans with the chickpeas in a large bowl. Add remaining ingredients and mix. Drain before serving.

Nutritional breakdown per serving

231 kcal – 975 KJ
Protein 14g
Fat 6g
Carbohydrates 32g

Especially high in most vitamins and minerals except B12 and D

Serves 1

1 banana
1 cup ice
2 fresh peaches *or*
   1 cup strawberries *or*
   1 cup blueberries *or*
   1 half-melon *or*
   1 pear *or*
   1 apple

A smoothie is a crushed blend of ice and fruit. You can combine any fruits, but adding a banana will always ensure a nice consistency.

Nutritional breakdown per serving

187 kcal – 1796 KJ
Protein 4g
Fat trace
Carbohydrates 45g

Especially high in vitamin C

Fruit with Fromage Frais

Serves 1–2

1 banana
1 papaya
½ cup seedless green grapes
½ cup strawberries
1 cup low-fat fromage frais

Cut fruit into small pieces and mix with fromage frais.

Nutritional breakdown per serving

338 kcal – 1438 KJ
Protein 13g
Fat 1g
Carbohydrates 74g

Especially high in vitamin C and calcium

Greek Salad

Serves 1–2

1 red pepper
1 orange pepper
1 cucumber, cubed
2 tomatoes, diced
2 tablespoons lemon juice
3 tablespoons red wine vinegar
¼ teaspoon dried oregano
2oz (60g) feta cheese

Mix peppers, cucumbers and tomatoes. Add lemon juice, vinegar and oregano, then the crumbled feta cheese.

Nutritional breakdown per serving

473 kcal – 1974 KJ
Protein 26g
Fat 13g
Carbohydrates 33g

Especially high in vitamins B6, folate, A, C and E

Green & Yellow Salad

Serves 1

2 cups (30g) spinach leaves, raw
2 cups (30g) rocket leaves
1 yellow sweet pepper, sliced
1 carrot, sliced
fresh corn from the cob
1 lemon
salt to taste

Steam corn separately and cut kernels off with a knife.
Combine spinach, rocket, pepper and carrot. Add corn
kernels. Sprinkle with lemon juice and salt to taste.
  This can be served with grilled fish.

Nutritional breakdown per serving

94 kcal – 400 KJ
Protein 4g
Fat 1.5g
Carbohydrates 17g

Especially high in folate, vitamins B6, A, C and E

Green Salad with Peanut & Sesame Dressing

Serves 4

mixture of green lettuces (spinach, rocket, little gem,
  lollo bianco, curly endive)
8oz (240g) asparagus
2oz (60g) mangetout
8oz (240g) broccoli cut into florets
½ fennel bulb, sliced
¼ cucumber, chopped

Wash lettuce leaves and place in salad bowl. Cut the tips
off the asparagus and plunge them into boiling water
with the mangetout, broccoli and fennel for 3 minutes.
Drain and refresh in cold water, then add to the lettuce
with the chopped cucumber. Whisk together all dressing ingredients and pour over salad. Toss well to mix,
and serve immediately.

Sliced baked chicken breast can be added to this dish.

Dressing

½ tablespoon (15ml) peanut butter
1 tablespoon water
1 teaspoon (5ml) sesame oil
½ tablespoon (15ml) cider vinegar
salt and pepper

Nutritional breakdown per serving

88 kcal – 364 KJ
Protein 7g
Fat 4g
Carbohydrates 5g

Especially high in folate and vitamin C

Serves 4

½ cup oats
½ cup rye flakes
½ cup barley flakes
1 banana, sliced
¼ cup sweet ready-made cereal for topping
1 cup skimmed milk

Mix grain flakes with fruit, add milk and sprinkle with ready-made cereal.

Nutritional breakdown per serving

392 kcal – 1671 KJ
Protein 13g
Fat 6g
Carbohydrates 77g

Especially high in all the B vitamins and almost all vitamins and minerals except A and D

Serves 4

4 medium potatoes (16oz/480g)
1–2 green chillies
1 onion
1 teaspoon turmeric
salt
1 tablespoon safflower oil
1½ teaspoons cumin seeds
5 curry leaves

Peel potatoes and cut into small cubes. Halve chillies, discard seeds and chop. Peel and chop onion. Boil the peeled potatoes with turmeric and salt for 10 minutes. Drain.

Heat oil and fry cumin, curry leaves and chillies for one minute. Add onion and fry for one minute. Add onion and fry for 10 minutes until golden. Add potatoes. Cook until tender.

Nutritional breakdown per serving

131 kcal – 551 KJ
Protein 3g
Fat 4g
Carbohydrates 22g

Especially high in vitamins B1, B6, C, E and folate

Serves 4

1lb (480g) spaghetti
2 peeled garlic cloves
3 small red chillies or more
1 teaspoon virgin olive oil
6 fresh tomatoes, chopped

Boil a large pan of salted water. Add pasta and cool until *al dente*. Chop garlic and chillies into small pieces and drop them into a pan containing a thin layer of hot olive oil. Don't scorch garlic: cook until medium brown. Drain pasta and place in pan with garlic, fresh tomatoes and chillies. Toss until slippery.

Nutritional breakdown per serving

447 kcal – 1900 KJ
Protein 15g
Fat 4g
Carbohydrates 93g

Especially high in vitamin C

Juicy Fruit with Cottage Cheese

Serves 1

½ 4 cup fresh blueberries
1 nectarine
½ cup seedless grapes
4oz (120g) cottage cheese

Cut berries and grapes in half, slice the nectarine, then mix with the cottage cheese.

Nutritional breakdown per serving

256 kcal – 1087 KJ
Protein 2g
Fat 20g
Carbohydrates 42g

Especially high in vitamin C (contrary to popular belief, cottage cheese is not high in calcium)

Lemon Potatoes

Serves 2

1½–2lb potatoes, peeled and diced
½oz (15g) butter or margarine
1–2 teaspoons finely grated lemon rind
salt and pepper

Boil the potatoes until tender, drain away any excess water, then toss in the butter, the lemon rind to taste, and season.

Add rosemary to the butter and lemon rind mixture.

Nutritional breakdown per serving

247 kcal – 1041 KJ
Protein 6g
Fat 7g
Carbohydrates 44g

Especially high in vitamins B1, B6, folate and C

Serves 1–3

4oz (120g) brown lentils/split peas
4oz (120g) chopped onion
1 crushed garlic clove
½ vegetable stock cube
2 teaspoons fresh basil, chopped
salt and pepper

Cook lentils or split peas in water with vegetable cubes until very soft paste. Add onion, garlic and seasoning, then simmer.

Nutritional breakdown per serving

541 kcal – 1830 KJ
Protein 15g
Fat 1g
Carbohydrates 132g

Especially high in iron and vitamin B1

Low-fat Yoghurt with Oat & Barley Flakes

Serves 4

½ cup low-fat yoghurt
½ cup oats
½ cup barley flakes

Mix grain flakes with yoghurt.

Nutritional breakdown per serving

220 kcal – 932 KJ
Protein 8g
Fat 41g
Carbohydrates 4g

Especially high in most vitamins and minerals except vitamins C, A, D and B12

Serves 6

2 egg whites
½ cup brown sugar

Almond Cream

¼ cup low-fat cottage cheese
1 tablespoon plain yoghurt
1 teaspoon almond flavouring
½ teaspoon vanilla flavouring
1½ teaspoons honey
12oz (360g) strawberries, sliced
4oz (120g) blueberries, cut in half

Lightly grease two oven trays and cover with grease-proof paper. Beat egg whites in small bowl until soft peaks form. Add the sugar gradually and beat until dissolved between each addition. Spoon into large piping bag fitted with a tube. Pipe swirls of mixture on to a prepared tray. Bake in a slow oven for two hours or until firm to the touch. Cool on trays. Add almond cream. To make cream, press cottage cheese through a fine sieve into a small bowl, stir in yoghurt, honey, vanilla and almond. Cover with berries.

Nutritional breakdown per serving

134 kcal – 573 KJ
Protein 3g
Fat 0
Carbohydrates 33g

Especially high in vitamin C

Serves 4

⅓ cup dried split peas
⅓ cup dried lentils
⅓ cup pearl barley
1 vegetable bouillon cube
7 cups water
6 small fresh tomatoes
2½ cups fresh carrots and/or celery
2 teaspoons dried basil
1½ teaspoons dried oregano
2 bay leaves
1 teaspoon chopped garlic
½ teaspoon pepper

Boil water and bouillon cube until dissolved. Wash peas, lentils and barley and mix with water. Bring to the boil, then cover and reduce heat. Simmer for 30 minutes. Add vegetables and spices. Simmer for 45–60 minutes until peas are tender. Remove the bay leaves.

Nutritional breakdown per serving

257 kcal – 1091 KJ
Protein 13g
Fat 2g
Carbohydrates 50g

Especially high in vitamins B1, B6, A and E

Serves 2

2 cups okra (ladiesfingers)
4 fresh tomatoes, chopped
1 can tomatoes
1 small onion
1 teaspoon garlic, chopped
salt and pepper to taste

Simmer tomatoes, okra, onion and seasoning until the okra is tender.

This can be served with lamb or lean beef.

Nutritional breakdown per serving

141 kcal – 598 KJ
Protein 11g
Fat 3g
Carbohydrates 20g

Especially high in folate, all the B vitamins, A, C and E

Oriental Broccoli

Serves 1

1 stalk of broccoli
1 cup mangetout
1 tablespoon soy sauce

Steam broccoli and mangetout for 10 minutes, uncovered. Drain water and place in dish. Add soy sauce.

Nutritional breakdown per serving

88 kcal – 369 KJ
Protein 11g
Fat 1g
Carbohydrates 8g

Especially high in folate and vitamin C

Serves 1

½ teaspoon pepper
½ teaspoon garlic powder
3oz (90g) angel hair pasta
¾ cup thinly sliced mushrooms
½ cup thinly sliced carrot

Boil water. Add the garlic and pepper, then the mushrooms and carrots and boil for 10 minutes. Add angel hair pasta, cook for 5 minutes. Serve.

Nutritional breakdown per serving

162 kcal – 682 KJ
Protein 7g
Fat 2g
Carbohydrates 31g

Especially high in vitamin A and folate

Serves 4

24oz (720g) young broad beans
12oz (360g) young peas, fresh
8oz (240g) asparagus
12–15 chervil sprigs or 8–10 basil leaves
6–8 parsley leaves
salt and pepper
1–2 chopped garlic cloves
1 cup fresh okra, chopped
8oz (240g/1 cup) spaghetti

Remove the thin skin from each broad bean. Add them to the peas. Snap off tough asparagus ends and slice the rest diagonally. Cook with the beans and peas for 10 seconds in plenty of salted water at a boil, then drain in a sieve. Bring a pan of salt water to a rolling boil. Heat the garlic gently with the oil in a shallow pan. Put the pasta into the boiling water. Put the vegetables into the garlic and oil and stew slowly, then season. Drain pasta and place in a warm bowl with vegetables and oil and the herbs.

A baked chicken breast can be added to this dish.

Nutritional breakdown per serving

427 kcal – 1796 KJ
Protein 26g
Fat 5g
Carbohydrates 72g

Especially high in vitamins B1, B6, folate, C and E

Serves 4

1lb (480g/2 cups) penne or tube pasta
2 cloves garlic
1 mild red chilli, split lengthways
1 teaspoon virgin olive oil
40–50 rocket leaves, stems removed
10 ripe plum tomatoes, chopped
140g fresh Parmesan

Boil a large pan of water with salt and add pasta. Cook until *al dente*. Crush the garlic so that it stays in one piece and place along with the whole split chilli into a thin layer of hot olive oil in a medium-sized pan. When the garlic turns medium brown, drop in most of the rocket leaves. As soon as the rocket looks like sautéed spinach, add tomatoes. Cook at a moderate heat for 5 minutes. Remove the garlic and chilli. Drain pasta and add sauce and Parmesan. Decorate with rocket leaves.

Nutritional breakdown per serving

499 kcal – 2120 KJ
Protein 19g
Fat 7g
Carbohydrates 95g

Especially high in vitamin C

Provençal Salad

Serves 4

½–1oz (20g) pine nuts
4oz (120g) French beans
11½oz (350g) artichoke hearts, canned
4oz (120g) button mushrooms
2oz (60g) radish
6½oz (200g) lettuce
1½oz (50g) oak leaf lettuce
1½oz (50g) curly endive
8oz (240g) tomatoes

Cut the artichokes, mushrooms, radish and beans into thin slices. Mix the lettuce, oak leaf lettuce and endive. Cut and dice tomatoes.

Place a hollow cylindrical can or container in the middle of a plate. Put the tomatoes in the bottom and add the rest of the vegetables in layers, the heaviest on the bottom and the pine nuts on top. Carefully remove the container.

Make a vinaigrette with extra-virgin olive oil, vinegar, a tiny bit of mustard and a tinge of fresh basil and tarragon.

Nutritional breakdown per serving

84 kcal – 351 KJ
Protein 5g
Fat 4g
Carbohydrates 7g

Especially high in folate and vitamin C

Serves 4

1 cup red kidney beans, cooked
½ cup barley
1 corn on the cob
1½ teaspoons chopped garlic
6 tomatoes
1 cup water (if using canned beans)
1 teaspoon chilli powder
1 teaspoon dried basil
1 teaspoon dried oregano
½ teaspoon pepper
1 teaspoon cumin
1 cup chopped carrots
1 cup chopped celery
1 medium onion

Combine ingredients, except for the corn on the cob, in a saucepan. Bring to the boil. Reduce heat and simmer, covered, for 20 minutes. Steam the corn on the cob separately and cut the kernels off with a knife.

For extra calcium and a thicker texture, you can add skimmed milk in place of some water.

Nutritional breakdown per serving

241 kcal – 1025 KJ
Protein 10g
Fat 3g
Carbohydrates 48g

Especially high in B vitamins, A and C

Red Pepper Couscous

Serves 6

1 cup (720g) couscous, cooked
1 carrot, julienned
1 cucumber, julienned
1 red pepper, cubed
1 tablespoon vinegar
1 teaspoon olive oil
1 tablespoon lemon juice
1 teaspoon salt

Place couscous in a large bowl and cover with boiling water. Let it stand for 10 minutes. Drain in a fine strainer then rinse under cold water. Add carrot, cucumber and red pepper and mix well. Add vinegar, olive oil, lemon and salt. Serve chilled.

Nutritional breakdown per serving

295 kcal – 1231 KJ
Protein 7g
Fat 3g
Carbohydrates 64g

Especially high in iron, B vitamins, A and C

Serves 4

3 peeled garlic cloves
1 teaspoon virgin olive oil
3½ pints (2l) water
7oz (210g) red split lentils
salt and pepper
8oz (240g) rocket, including stems

Crack the garlic cloves then heat the oil in a large
saucepan and fry the garlic over a very low heat for
2–3 minutes or until a deep brown. Add water, and boil.
Add lentils and simmer, covered, for 10 minutes. Season, add rocket, cover and simmer for 2 more minutes.

Nutritional breakdown per serving

191 kcal – 87 KJ
Protein 13g
Fat 3g
Carbohydrates 31g

Especially high in vitamin B1, iron and folate

Serves 1

rocket leaves
2 red peppers, sliced
1 cucumber, sliced
1 lemon
salt to taste

Combine rocket leaves, sliced red peppers and cucumber. Add lemon juice and salt to taste.
This can be served with grilled fish.

Nutritional breakdown per serving

117 kcal – 486 KJ
Protein 5g
Fat 2g
Carbohydrates 21g

Especially high in vitamins A, C and folate

Serves 2

Gnocchi

1½lb (720g/3 cups) floury potatoes
1 beaten egg
½ teaspoon salt
1oz (30g) rocket, chopped at the last minute
7oz (200g) flour

Topping

24 cherry tomatoes
salt and pepper
1 tablespoon butter
1oz (30g) shaved Parmesan

To make the gnocchi: cook the potatoes in their skins in boiling salted water until tender. As soon as they are cool enough to handle, peel them, then return to the pan and place over a gentle heat for 1–2 minutes, shaking the pan to evaporate any leftover water and slightly break up the potatoes. Mash thoroughly: begin with a conventional potato masher and finish with a wire whisk.

Whisk egg in with salt, then the chopped rocket.

With a wooden spoon add flour to make a soft, sticky dough. Heat oven to 400°F (200°C, Gas mark 6). Cut the tomatoes in half, place in one layer on a baking sheet and season. Bake for 20 minutes or until hot and bubbling. Shape the dough into long sausages as thick as your thumb, then cut into 1-inch (2.5cm) lengths. Boil a large pan of salt water and drop in gnocchi in batches of 15. They will rise quickly to the surface. Simmer for 10 seconds and then remove with a slotted spoon to a heated dish. Melt butter in a small pan. Mix the gnocchi, tomatoes and butter together and divide into 6 servings. Add Parmesan.

Nutritional breakdown per serving

461 kcal – 18 KJ
Protein 18g
Fat 15g
Carbohydrates 66g

Especially high in vitamins A, C, B6, B1 and folate

Spiced Rice

Serves 4

2 cups water
pinch dried rosemary
¼ teaspoon dried marjoram
¼ teaspoon dried thyme
1 teaspoon dried onion
1 cup quick cooking brown rice

Mix first five ingredients in a saucepan. Bring to the boil. Add the rice, reduce heat and simmer for 15 minutes.

Nutritional breakdown per serving

219 kcal – 930 KJ
Protein 4g
Fat 2g
Carbohydrates 50g

Especially high in vitamin B1, folate and copper

Spicy Sesame Noodles

Serves 4

2 tablespoons sesame oil
2 tablespoons dried crushed red pepper
5 tablespoons soy sauce
1 tablespoon tahini
1 teaspoon peanut butter
2oz (60g) cooked noodles (spaghetti or flat in circles)
1 teaspoon toasted sesame seeds
1 tablespoon chopped peanuts
1 big cucumber, julienned
1 red pepper, cubed

Place oil in pan on a very low heat. Add pepper and continue heating to bring out flavour. Add soy, salt, tahini and peanut butter. Stir slowly to combine ingredients, then set aside.

Cook noodles until tender, drain and combine with mixture.

Add cucumber, red pepper, peanuts and sesame seeds. Serve hot, or cover and refrigerate to serve cold.

Nutritional breakdown per serving

250 kcal – 1045 KJ
Protein 8g
Fat 14g
Carbohydrates 25g

Especially high in vitamin C

Spinach & Barley Soup

Serves 2

½ cup barley
3 cups water
1 onion, chopped
1 clove garlic, chopped
2 carrots, diced
1 head/stalk celery, diced
1 potato, diced
5 tomatoes, diced
1 vegetable stock cube

Soak barley in water overnight. Heat oil in a large saucepan, add onion and garlic, stir over medium heat for 2 minutes or until onion is soft. Add vegetables and stock. Bring to the boil, then reduce heat and simmer for 15 minutes until the vegetables are tender.

For extra calcium and a thicker texture, you can add skimmed milk in place of some water.

Nutritional breakdown per serving

281 kcal – 1193 KJ
Protein 8g
Fat 2g
Carbohydrates 61g

Especially high in vitamins B1, B6, folate, iron, C, A and E

Spinach & Fresh Pea Salad

Serves 4

spinach leaves
1 tomato
1 cucumber
1 cup watercress, chopped
1 cup fresh peas, shelled
1 lemon
salt to taste

Combine ingredients. Add lemon and salt to taste.
Cubed lean ham can be added.

Nutritional breakdown per serving

105 kcal – 435 KJ
Protein 10g
Fat 3g
Carbohydrates 11g

Especially high in vitamins B, A, C and folate

Spinach & Pea Salad

Serves 2

2 cups (60g) spinach
1 cup freshly shelled peas, raw
1 tablespoon lemon juice
1 teaspoon salt
1 chopped tomato

Nutritional breakdown per serving

294 kcal – 1231 KJ
Protein 28g
Fat 6g
Carbohydrates 13g

Especially high in vitamins A, C, E, B1, B6 and folate

Serves 4

1 cup green split peas
1 cup fresh spinach, chopped
4 cups water
1 lemon
salt and pepper to taste

Cook split peas and water until soft. Bring to the boil. Reduce heat and simmer, covered, for 40 minutes. Stir in spinach and cook for 10 minutes. Add lemon juice, salt and pepper to taste.

Lean bacon or ham can be added.

Nutritional breakdown per serving

213 kcal – 902 KJ
Protein 2g
Fat 2g
Carbohydrates 36g

Especially high in almost all vitamins and minerals except B12 and D

Serves 1–2

1¼lb (550g/2½ cups) spinach, chopped
1 teaspoon nutmeg
2 tablespoons lemon juice
salt and pepper

Cook the spinach. Stir in the nutmeg and lemon juice, and season.

This can be used either as a dip or as a dressing for vegetables.

Nutritional breakdown per serving

152 kcal – 627 KJ
Protein 18g
Fat 7g
Carbohydrates 10g

Especially high in iron, calcium and folate

Three-bean Soup

Serves 4

1 cup mung beans
1 cup lentils
1 cup adzuki beans
1½ teaspoons chopped garlic
6 tomatoes
7 cups water
1 teaspoon chilli powder
1 teaspoon dried basil
1 teaspoon dried oregano
½ teaspoon pepper
1 teaspoon cumin
1 cup chopped carrots
1 cup chopped celery
1 medium onion

Combine dried beans and water. Bring to the boil. Reduce heat and simmer, covered, for 30 minutes. Stir in vegetables and seasoning and cook for 15–20 minutes.

Nutritional breakdown per serving

428 kcal – 1878 KJ
Protein 30g
Fat 2g
Carbohydrates 77g

Especially high in B vitamins, A and C

Serves 1–2

¾ cup (6oz/180g) pizza sauce
1oz grated low-fat mozzarella cheese
1oz low-fat Cheddar cheese
2 baguettes
¼ cup sliced mushrooms
½ cup sliced red peppers
¼ cup fresh spinach
⅛ cup jalapeno peppers

Pre-heat oven to 475°F. Cut baguettes in half and spread pizza sauce on each half. Add cheese and vegetables. Bake for 15 minutes.

Half a cup of lean minced beef can be added to the pizza topping.

Nutritional breakdown per serving

785 kcal – 3325 KJ
Protein 42g
Fat 19g
Carbohydrates 118g

Especially high in most vitamins and minerals except D, E, B12 and zinc

Tomato & Basil Purée

Serves 1–2

1 teaspoon olive oil
8oz (240g/½ cup) chopped onion
2 crushed garlic cloves
1½lb (720g) ripe chopped tomatoes
3 tablespoons tomato paste
1½ tablespoons chopped fresh basil
salt and black pepper

Heat the oil and fry onion until soft. Add the garlic, tomatoes, tomato paste and basil and mix. Cook, uncovered, until the tomatoes are soft and the mixture is reduced to a thick purée, then season. This makes a good dip or dressing for vegetables.

Nutritional breakdown per serving

343 kcal – 1454 KJ
Protein 13g
Fat 10g
Carbohydrates 56g

Especially high in vitamin C

Serves 2

2 large tomatoes, diced
fresh basil
1 teaspoon chopped garlic
½ teaspoon salt
pepper
6oz (180g) angel hair pasta

Mix tomatoes with seasonings and basil and let sit at room temperature. Cook the pasta then drain it and add the tomato mixture.

Nutritional breakdown per serving

323 kcal – 1377 KJ
Protein 11g
Fat 2g
Carbohydrates 69g

Especially high in vitamins B1, C and folate

Serves 1–2

6oz (180g/1 cup) onion, chopped
6oz (180g/1 cup) sliced celery
6oz (180g/1 cup) diced red pepper
6oz (180g/1 cup) diced carrots
2 crushed garlic cloves
½ vegetable bouillon cube
8oz (240g) can chopped tomatoes
1½ tablespoons fresh parsley, chopped
¼ cup (60g) grated Cheddar cheese
salt and pepper
1 teaspoon grated lemon rind
2 teaspoons chopped fresh marjoram

Set oven to 375°F (190°C/Gas mark 5). Steam the
vegetables and garlic, covered, for 10 minutes or until
soft, then mix in the stock cube. Stir in the tomatoes and
cook for 5 minutes uncovered. Add the lemon rind and
herbs and cook uncovered for 3 more minutes. Stir in
half the cheese, then season. Place the mixture in a 2
pint/1 litre casserole dish and top with the remaining
cheese. Bake for 20–30 minutes until the topping is
melted and browned.

Nutritional breakdown per serving

500 kcal – 2090 KJ
Protein 25g
Fat 24g
Carbohydrates 50g

Especially high in vitamins B1, B6, folate, A, C and E

Serves 1–2

2 large tomatoes, sliced
fresh basil
1 teaspoon chopped garlic
½ teaspoon salt
pepper
1 lemon

Mix ingredients and let sit at room temperature.

Nutritional breakdown per serving

33 kcal – 142 KJ
Protein 2g
Fat ½g
Carbohydrates 6g

Especially high in vitamins C, A and E

Tomato Soup

Serves 2

8 fresh tomatoes
1 14oz (400g) can tomatoes
1 cup water
1 teaspoon dried basil
1 teaspoon pepper
salt to taste

Combine ingredients. Bring to the boil. Reduce heat and simmer, covered, for 15 minutes.

For extra calcium and a thicker texture, you can add skimmed milk in place of some water.

Nutritional breakdown per serving

189 kcal – 873 KJ
Protein 10g
Fat 3g
Carbohydrates 35g

Especially high in vitamins B1, B6, folate, A, C and E

Tropical Cottage Cheese

Serves 1

1 banana
1 papaya
4oz (120g) low-fat cottage cheese

Cut berries and grapes in half, slice the nectarine, then mix with a small container of cottage cheese.

Nutritional breakdown per serving

258 kcal – 1095 KJ
Protein 18g
Fat 2g
Carbohydrates 44g

Especially high in vitamin C

Serves 2

1 vegetable bouillon cube
pinch dried basil
pinch dried thyme
¼ teaspoon dried onion
2 cups chopped fresh vegetables (potatoes, corn, broc-
    coli, carrots, etc.)
3 cups water

Boil 1½ cups water in a saucepan with bouillon cube.
Add basil, thyme and onion. Add vegetables. Cover and
cook until vegetables are tender.

For extra calcium and a thicker texture, you can add
skimmed milk in place of some water.

Nutritional breakdown per serving

172 kcal – 1725 KJ
Protein 7g
Fat 2g
Carbohydrates 34g

Especially high in vitamins C, A, B1, B6 and folate

Serves 2

1 tablespoon sesame seeds
6 small yellow squashes
1 teaspoon olive oil
1 small onion, chopped
1 teaspoon light soy sauce
1 clove garlic, crushed

Stir sesame seeds over low heat in an ungreased frying pan to brown them. Remove. Boil or steam the squash until tender. Scoop a hole in the top of each squash. Cube the part you remove. In a small saucepan, heat oil, onion and garlic for 2 minutes. Add the chopped squash and soy sauce and cook for 1 minute.

Spoon the mixture into the squash, then heat in a warm oven for 10 minutes.

Nutritional breakdown per serving

131 kcal – 544 KJ
Protein 3g
Fat 7g
Carbohydrates 13g

Especially high in vitamins B1 and C

BIBLIOGRAPHY

Clark, Nancy, *Nancy Clark's Sports Nutrition Guidebook*, Leisure Press, Champaign, Illinois, 1990.

Whitney, Eleanor Noss, Cataldo, Corine Balog and Rolfes, Sharon Rady, *Understanding Normal and Clinical Nutrition*, West Publishing Company, New York, 1987.

Further Reading

Bean, Anita, *The Complete Guide to Sports Nutrition*, A&C Black, 1996.

Bovey, Shelley, *Being Fat is Not a Sin*, Pandora, 1994.

Clark, Nancy, *Nancy Clark's Sports Nutrition Guidebook*, Leisure Press, 1990.

Hunking, Penny, *Energise for Exercise Workbook* (available from 01483 728480).

Town and Kearney, *Swim, Bike, Run*, Human Kinetics, 1993.

Vartabedian, Dr Roy E. and Matthews, Kathy, *Nutripoints*, Grafton Press, 1996.

Wolf, Naomi, *The Beauty Myth*, Vintage, 1991.

FURTHER INFORMATION

For information on Martica's books and videos contact Mind & Muscle, PO Box 363, London, WC2H 9BW or phone (0171) 240 9861.

Penny Hunking, SRD, the nutritional consultant for this book, is dedicated to raising the awareness of good nutrition within an active lifestyle. Penny runs her own company, Re-Energise, offering nutritional conventions and a comprehensive range of Energise nutritional products and services. For more information contact: Energise, PO Box 244, Woking, Surrey GU22 7FD.